D0089035

PORTRAIT OF THE SCOTT COUNTRY

Portrait of
THE SCOTT COUNTRY

MARION LOCHHEAD

ILLUSTRATED
AND WITH MAP

ROBERT HALE · LONDON

© *Marion Lockhead 1968 and 1973*
First published in Great Britain 1968
Second edition 1973
Reprinted 1976

ISBN 0 7091 3957 8

Robert Hale & Company
Clerkenwell House
Clerkenwell Green
London EC1R oHT

Printed in Great Britain by
Lowe & Brydone (Printers) Ltd, Thetford, Norfolk

CONTENTS

ILLUSTRATIONS

ACKNOWLEDGEMENTS

The author and publishers wish to thank the following
for permission to reproduce the above illustrations:
Roy Birks (Nos. 8, 26); The British Travel and
Holiday Association (2); Scottish Television Limited
(3), G. Douglas Bolton (20, 21); A. D. S. Mac-
pherson (6, 9, 18, 27); A. Walker and Son Limited
(10, 19); David Hope (11); Frank H. Meads (28);
Hector Innes (12, 13, 14, 15); L. S. Paterson (16, 24);
Fred G. Sykes (17, 23); W. A. Sharp (22); British
Broadcasting Corporation, photo. by R. L.
Williamson Studios (25); The Tweeddale Press
Limited (1, 4, 5, 7).

To
Patricia and Jean
Maxwell-Scott
of Abbotsford
with love
and gratitude

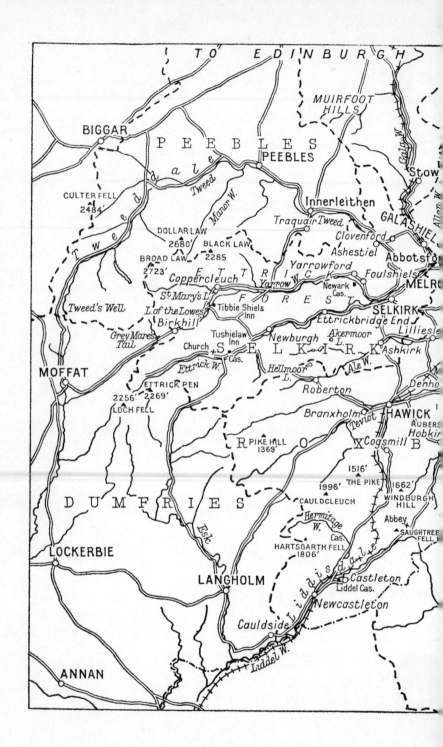

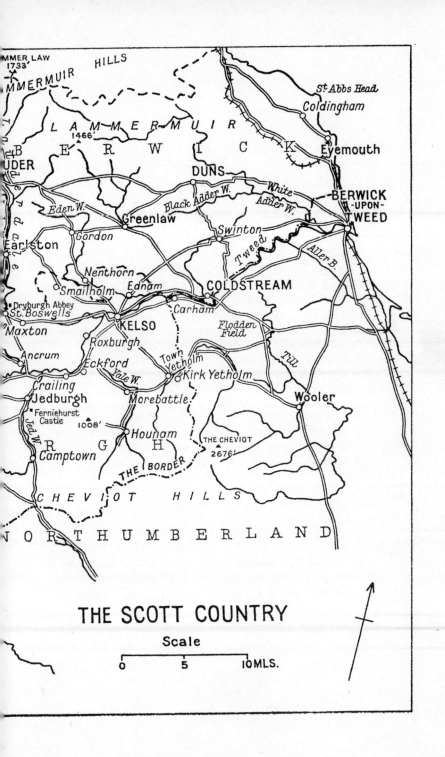

MMER LAW
1733'

MMERMUIR HILLS

St Abbs Head
Coldingham

LAMMERMUIR

BERWICK

1466'

UDER

Eyemouth

DUNS

Eden W.

Black Adder W.

White Adder W.

BERWICK
-UPON-
TWEED

Greenlaw

Earlston

Gordon

Swinton

Tweed

Aller B.

Nenthorn

Ednam

COLDSTREAM

Smailholm

Dryburgh Abbey
St.Boswells

Carham

Flodden
Field

Maxton

KELSO

Roxburgh

Till

Ancrum

Eckford

Vale W.

Town
Yetholm

Crailing

Kirk Yetholm

Jedburgh

Morebattle

Ferniehurst
Castle   1008'

Wooler

Jed W.

Hounam

THE CHEVIOT
2676'

R   G   H

Camptown

THE BORDER

CHEVIOT   HILLS

NORTHUMBERLAND

THE SCOTT COUNTRY

Scale

0   5   10MLS.

ACKNOWLEDGEMENTS

I am grateful to the following for the use of copyright material:

The University of Edinburgh, and the Reverend Dr. James Bulloch and Mr. Ian Urquhart for the Peebles and Selkirk volume in the *Third Statistical Account of Scotland*;

The Scotsman, The Border Telegraph, the Tweeddale Press and Mr. Edwin Hector; *The Scots Magazine* and Mr. Tom Todd; *Scotland's Magazine* and Mr. Matt Rundell for newspaper and magazine reports and articles;

Mr. Stewart Cruden for *The Scottish Abbeys*;

Susan Lady Tweedsmuir and Messrs. A. P. Watt & Son for John Buchan's books, Kathleen Fidler and the Lutterworth Press for *Flash the Sheep Dog*.

My thanks go also to Messrs. Alex. Walker and Son, Galashiels, and to the Abbotsford Mills there, for so kindly showing me over their respective printing works and factory;

To Mr. Ian Nimmo who sent me on this journey through The Scott Country, and to Mr. Gordon Chesterfield who encouraged my progress; and to Mrs. and Miss Maxwell-Scott for manifold help and kindness.

My debt to the National Library of Scotland increases, and is the more happily acknowledged for the fact that the Librarian, Professor Beattie, and the Keeper of Manuscripts, Mr. William Park, are both good Borderers.

I

SCOTT AND HIS COUNTRY

> He loved the twilight that surrounds
> The borderland of old romance . . .
> . . . The dusk of centuries and of song.
> Longfellow

THE genius and personality of Sir Walter Scott have given his name to the part of Scotland he knew best, loved most, and made known and loved by countless others long after his own day. The name is almost but not quite synonymous with the Borders. It does not include the south-west, Dumfries and Galloway, although two of his greatest novels, *Guy Mannering* and *Redgauntlet* were to be set in that region, and *Old Mortality* in Clydesdale; Berwickshire and Peeblesshire are, as it were, the frame to the portrait, a frame which is almost a part of the composition. The true Scott countries are Selkirkshire and Roxburghshire; there much of his life from babyhood was spent; there, in Selkirk, lay his shrievedom, at Abbotsford his home. Tweed is his river above all, Ettrick, Teviot and Yarrow with their many tributaries coming very close after it in his affection. The Eildons, Muirfoot, Lammermuirs, Dunian, Rubislaw, Cheviot are his hills. It is hill country, river and pastoral valley in a pattern that cannot be surpassed for intimate beauty, a quality which holds the heart; clear country, the brooding darkness of the hills and some of the valleys lit by the brilliance of running water, for it is river rather than loch or lake land. There are higher, more majestic mountains in the north, but the average height here is among the highest in Scotland.

The Borders may indeed claim to be the most complex part of Scotland in both scenery and character. Other regions may equal or surpass them in beauty; the West Highlands have an almost unearthly loveliness, and match them in history and tradition.

There are towns as historic as the Border towns, and many that are larger, cities full of a teeming life not to be found here. But nowhere is there such a varied and intricate pattern of life, past and present, history, poetry, modern activity or one so inextricably interwoven.

River and pastoral country, the hills in the background never far from sight, the busy towns, even Hawick and Galashiels the most bustling and absorbed in industry are close to the country, neighboured by villages. There are farms, mixed and agricultural in the valleys, sheep-farms on the uplands. Sheep indeed make the fortune of the Borders, and sheep-farming here has no such cruel history as it has in many parts of the Highlands where it meant evictions, the enforced exile of men from the land of their fathers, to make room for flocks.

Pastoral country, it has for the most part a peaceful beauty, a pensive grace which Dorothy Wordsworth, the poet's sister, noted and loved. The hills stand around the fields and rivers protectively; they can be dark and rough and terrible with storm, they have their legends, but they do not have the tragic, brooding majesty of the Highland bens. Their memories are bearable.

Every element of natural beauty is here except the sea, and there is no lack of water, still or running, in loch and burn and river. Hills and trees, fields green or golden, water silvery bright or glinting brown, stillness and rippling motion, gentleness and dignity, fruitfulness and solitude all these must be near or present to compose a complete and satisfying landscape, and in this Border country we find them all.

The colours are subtle.

"The prevailing colour of upper Tweeddale is tawny", George Burnett has written in his pleasant *Companion to Tweed*; even in spring, still more in autumn this warmth is present. But it is green too, in a multiplicity of tones, at all times; green of grass and of leaf, with the varying enrichment of flowers from the first delicacy of yellow and white to the late purple and gold and russet of autumn, in heather and bracken. Living colour, living water, living light fill the scene.

The very names make poetry. The rivers run pleasantly in sound: Tweed and Till, Teviot and Yarrow, Gala and Eden, Ale and Manor Water, Leader and Ettrick. Town and place-names match them: Abbotsford and Huntly Burn, Chiefswood and

Darnick, Traquair, Fairnilee, Yair; Melrose, most mellifluous of town-names, Jedburgh or Jeddart or Jedworth, Kelso, Selkirk; and the hills ring out like a peal of music: Eildon, Dunion, Muirfoot, Rubislaw. These hills are part of the pre-history of the Borders; this country is truly as old as the hills.

They rise in height from 500 to 2,500 above sea level, most of them green and rounded. John Buchan, a good Borderer by upbringing—though over to the west, in Peeblesshire, wrote of "the grey hills that cradle Tweed"; a phrase strangely inaccurate from a lover, for there is colour everywhere, subtle and pervasive. These are no more grey hills than is the western region grey Galloway.

Geologically the land is ancient; centuries old in history, in tradition, its past is hidden in pre-history with only such traces as the rocks can give. It is mainly Silurian, in parts Ordovician. Once the land lay under ocean, then under ice. The slow but ceaseless action of glaciers, wind, rain and streams shaped those hills, producing what another Borderer, Professor Veitch, called "wavy lines of hills as if arrested in water-flow". They have made this region show "the sculpture of the unseen powers of those long gone years".

The country was once thickly wooded:

> Ettrick Foreste is a fair foreste,
> In it grows many a seemly tree;
> There's hart and hind and deer and raw [roe]
> And of a' wild bestis grete plentie

—as it is said in "The Ballad of the Outlaw Murray".

In time the woods grew thin, many of the trees destroyed, until, in the early nineteenth century, an English traveller could describe the Border scenery baldly thus: "a hill, a road, and a tree".

There has been, happily, new planting and afforestation; but it remains a country of hill and river more than of woodlands.

This book or portrait was begun in Scott's own house of Abbotsford on the Tweed, its windows looking upon the river he loved, Galashiels on the other side, Melrose about three miles away, the Eildons looking down on the landscape he chose for home. Portrait is the true word, for a portrait should reveal both a face and the character behind it, a personality and a background. This Border country is itself a personality.

The land helped to make Scott as he helped to make it famous beyond the bounds of Scotland, revealing its treasury of poetry and legend. It made him in spirit; this was the birthplace of his genius and imagination. He was born in Edinburgh and loved his own romantic town, had his schooling there, went to college, walked the floor of Parliament House as a young advocate, became Clerk to the Court of Session, lived with his wife and children in his own house in Castle Street and was for half his life and more one of the most notable figures in the old town and the new. But he was born again on his grandfather's farm of Sandyknowe near Smailholm in Roxburghshire, where, a small, lame boy of barely two, he was sent to recover from delicacy and deformity, in the pure country air, under the care of his grandmother and his Aunt Janet. Wrapped, like Baby Bunting, in a skin (a newly flayed sheepskin was an old cure for lameness) he was carried out to lie among the sheep on the hillside, under the eye of an old shepherd.

Years later he recalled this, in the fragment of Autobiography which Lockhart was to incorporate in his *Life of Sir Walter Scott*.

"It was here, at Sandyknowe . . . that I had the first consciousness of existence. . . . In this Tartar-like habiliment I well remember lying upon the floor of the little parlour in the farmhouse, while my grandfather, a venerable old man with white hair, used every excitement to make me try to crawl. . . . I was usually carried out and laid down beside the old shepherd among the crags or rocks round which he fed his sheep." He told his friend Skene that "the sort of friendship he thus formed with the sheep and lambs had impressed his mind with a degree of affectionate feeling towards them which had lasted throughout life".

John Geddie has truly said in his *Scott Country* that Edinburgh, the rest of Scotland and all the varied settings of the Waverley novels are "merely excursions of a spirit whose abiding home or favourite haunt was the valley of Tweed and its encircling hills"; Eildon rather than Arthur's seat being "the high place of the Scott cult". He would circumscribe the country within a small area: the meeting of Ettrick, Gala and Leader with Tweed, under the Eildons; little below Kelso, not much above Drummelzier. Teviot and Ettrick, Harden and Newark were his father's country, Jedburgh that of his mother's family, the Rutherfords, and here as a young lawyer he came to the Assizes. Yarrow "the heart of his

Abbotsford, floodlit for Scott's bi-centenary celebrations

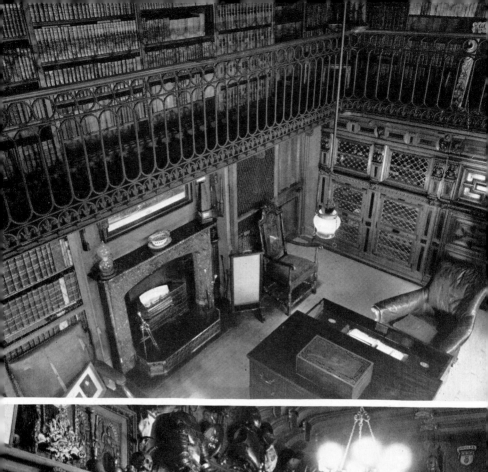

Forest Sheriffdom is also the core of his ballad poetry". At Kelso "we come fully within the circle of the Magician's charm—where every stream and wood and glen seem to take light and colour from the imagination of Walter Scott".

He was so many-sided, his life so intricate in its passions and activities. The boy, the young lawyer, the wandering ballad-hunter, the sheriff, the laird, the poet and novelist—all these persons grew and flourished in the country which now bears his name, like a kingdom.

To return to that first childhood at Sandyknowe, all his life he loved the pastoral country and he loved animals. "A sweet-tempered bairn", two old women remembered him, after his death. "A darling with all about the house, very gleg at the uptake, and soon kenned every sheep and lamb by headmark, as well as any of them." It was characteristic; he would, from boyhood onward always know people, as well as animals, separately by their headmark or personality, never seeing them in a mere mass.

He was well loved, with an occasional thrust of criticism.

"One may as well speak in the mouth of a cannon as where that child is", said the parish minister who when calling at the farm heard the small Walter reciting, full-voiced, the "Ballad of Hardy-knute."

His love of poetry and romance was derived from "the old songs and ballads which then formed the amusement of a retired country family"—so he recalled in his autobiography. "My grandfather, in whose youth the old Border depredations were matter of recent tradition, used to tell me many a tale of Wat of Harden"—their own ancestor—"and of other heroes, merrymen all, of the persuasion and calling of Robin Hood and Little John." Aunt Janet used to read to him from one of the old books that lay on the parlour window-seat. Their own family history was exciting enough for any boy. Wat of Harden—another Walter Scott—was a bold Border reiver, with a wife, Mary, so lovely that she was known as The Flower of Yarrow. Their son took after his father, and he, captured by the hostile clan of Murray of Elibank, was offered a choice between hanging and matrimony. Young Scott looked at the offered bride, Murray's daughter, a lady of little beauty known as Muckle-mou'ed Meg, and ungallantly chose the gallows. Later, by persuasion or upon reflection he changed his mind and married the lass. Even apart from saving his

Abbotsford: the study and entrance hall

life, he chose well. Meg made him a good wife; what she may
have lacked in looks she made up in sense and character. One of
their sons was Scott of Raeburn, and his son, another Walter, was
known as Beardie, from the long beard he refused to shave until a
Stuart King should come again to the throne. One of Beardie's
sons was Robert Scott of Sandyknowe, grandfather of our Walter
whose father the lawyer was the first of the family to take to a profession and town life rather than farming, sheep-rearing, and it
may be permissible to suggest, sheep-reiving. Or had old Robert
renounced such vanities?

From Sandyknowe the boy was taken to Bath, for the waters,
then home to Edinburgh to the house in George Square, to school
and family life. He came again to Sandyknowe between the ages
of seven and eight, more than ever receptive of atmosphere and
tradition. At twelve he spent some months in Kelso with Aunt
Janet, who, since her parents' death had lived there in a small
house with a large garden. Walter went to the Grammar School
where the master was one Lancelot Whale, a man of immense
height and immense learning, with more than a hint in him of
Dominie Sampson. A good teacher as well as a sound scholar, he
brought the boy on well in the classics he had neglected at
Edinburgh High School.

In Kelso he met the Ballantynes, James and John, with whose
fortunes and misfortunes his own were to be so lamentably intertwined. Here, as in the School Yard in Edinburgh, he won fame
as a teller of tales:

"Come slink over beside me, Jamie," he bade his friend, "and
I'll tell you a story." He read voraciously: poetry, romances, the
great eighteenth-century novels of Richardson, Fielding and
Smollet, and *The Man of Feeling* by Henry Mackenzie who would
become his friend. He even forgot dinner one day, as he sat reading
in the garden. And it was not only book learning that quickened
his powers:

"To this period too, I can trace distinctly the waking of that
delightful feeling for the beauties of natural objects which has
never since deserted me. The neighbourhood of Kelso, the most
beautiful if not the most romantic village in Scotland, is emi-
nently calculated to awaken those ideas. It presents objects not
only grand in themselves but venerable in their association. The
meeting of two superb rivers, the Tweed and the Teviot, both

renowned in song, the ruins of an ancient Abbey, the more distant vestiges of Roxburgh Castle, the modern mansion of Fleurs
. . . are in themselves objects of the first class, yet are so mixed,
united and melted among a thousand other beauties of a less
prominent description, that they harmonise into one picture. . . .
From this time, the love of natural beauty, more especially when
combined with ancient ruins or remains of our fathers' piety or
splendour, became with me an insatiable passion."

At this point we may recall Jane Austen's comment, in a letter
to her brother Francis, about their elder brother Henry's tour of
Scotland, in 1813: "He met with scenes of higher beauty in Roxburghshire than I had supposed the South of Scotland possessed".

English travellers, and readers of travel-journals were hardly
aware, yet, of the beauty of the Borders. The sense of the picturesque mingled with a love of romantic ruins, had been stirred
by Scott himself, and his poetry had made The Trossachs and the
Highlands famous among a multitude; but even he had not yet
conveyed the quiet and subtle charm of his own countryside.
Some of its treasury of poetry and ballads had been given to the
world in his *Border Minstrelsy*; in time his love of the Borders
would communicate itself to his readers.

Another friend of those Kelso days was Robert Waldie whose
family were Quakers, and who introduced young Walter to the
Friends; from them came the description of the Geddie household
in *Redgauntlet*.

After this visit he returned to Edinburgh, to the High School
and in due course, the University, then to the law office and to
Parliament House, always with a second home in Kelso with Aunt
Janet or with his Uncle Robert who also had a house there. He was
to develop that love of France which is part of the cultivated
Scottish mind, and Kelso has the air of a French town, elegant and
formal in pattern, set on its wide river with a noble bridge
(Rennie's prelude to the old Waterloo Bridge in London), with
a market square, an old abbey in the background, and a great
château. It was then as now a scene of busy provincial life, and for
all Scott's immense achievement one cannot help regretting some
omissions, sighing for the novels he did not write: those of *la vie
de province* in Scotland.

All his life he was to go on discovering this country of his heart,
in town and village, by hill and river. As a young advocate he

attended the Assizes at Jedburgh, and there met the Sheriff-Depute
of the county, Roxburgh, Robert Shortreed with whom he made
a strong friendship. They both loved the Borders, both loved old
tales and ballads, and forthwith began a series of peaceful raids
upon the countryside. They drove about in a gig, the first to be
seen in the remote parts of the valleys; where there was no inn
they stayed at the manse or a farm or in a shepherd's cottage,
delighted and delightful guests. Scott was a good companion. An
old shepherd struck the keynote of his character:

"He aye did as the lave did. . . . I've seen him in a' moods . . .
grave and gay, daft and serious, sober or drunk . . . but drunk or
sober, he was aye the gentleman."

From those raids he brought back the treasures of *The Border
Minstrelsy*. He met not only the shepherds and farmers and other
country folk but the gipsies in their own kingdom of Yetholm
in Roxburghshire; and so, many years later, presented Meg
Merrilees and her tribe.

Meanwhile in his private life he had met and lost his first love,
his true and lifelong love who left a wound in his heart, though he
did not pine or look bereft. She was Williamina Stuart-Belsches
whose parents had other ideas for her. Scott met and married
Charlotte Charpentier, his second love who made him a good
wife and brought him four dearly loved and loving children. They
set up house in Castle Street, Edinburgh, with a country cottage at
Lasswade on the Esk.

In his profession he made good progress, being appointed
Sheriff of Selkirk or, more accurately, of Ettrick Forest, in 1799;
it was his own country, and the appointment linked his private
and his official life together most agreeably, providing also a
stable income and position. The third aspect of his life was also
bright, that of the man of letters. For some time he had been
working on his collection of ballads and popular poetry and in
1801 published, with immense popular approbation, *The Border
Minstrelsy*. In this—as Andrew Lang has put it—"he glided from
law into literature" and into fame. His own romantic narrative
poems followed: *The Lay of the Last Minstrel* which has all the
glamourie of the Borders, *Marmion*, *The Lady of the Lake*—all the
vivid, galloping and often singing verse that captivated the literary world and many who made little pretence to book-learning,
holding them entranced for more than one generation to come.

He was living thus, between Edinburgh, Lasswade and his shrievedom when William and Dorothy Wordsworth called on him, on their way to Peebles, during their tour of Scotland in 1803. They, ten years before Henry Austen, perceived the beauty of the Borders. At Neidpath Castle Wordsworth mourned "the fallen woods" addressing a sonnet of reproof to "Degenerate Douglas"—the Duke of Queensberry who had been responsible for the neglect. But even a degenerate Duke could not spoil the loveliness of river and pastureland:

> The pure mountains and the gentle Tweed
> And the green, silent pastures yet remain.

Dorothy found the scene lovely enough even unwooded. They left Peebles on Sunday morning, at the hour when a throng of "well-dressed people were going to church", no doubt wondering who those ungodly strangers were. The Wordsworths had chosen to walk, sending their car or gig on before them. An inquisitive and suspicious townsman stopped them to ask whether they were Irish or foreign or what.

"I suppose our car was the object of suspicion at a time when everyone was talking of the threatened invasion" by Bonaparte's troops, during that long war with France; or it may have been merely Sabbatarian doubt of the respectability of people who went walking on the Sabbath in the opposite direction from the kirk.

Brother and sister walked on, along Tweed "a name which has been dear to my ears almost as far back as I can remember anything", through pastoral country with a few corn-fields, among the hills: gentle country, softly coloured:

"The hills, whether smooth or stony, uncultivated or covered with ripe corn, had the same pensive softness". It had a prosperous look, too, some of the large farms with their steadings being almost like small villages.

"It was a clear, autumnal day without wind, and being Sunday, the business of the harvest was suspended, and all that we saw and felt and heard combined to excite our sensation of pensive and still pleasure."

It is part of the charm of the Borders that the perceptions of the different senses become a unity, a fusion; the colour of hills and fields, trees and flowers and water, the shape of the hills, the ripple

of the river, the sound of wind in the trees, bird-song and the
bleating of sheep, the scent of earth and grass all appear to merge
into one sensation, as if all the gateways of the senses made one
wide entry into the mind and imagination. There is this magic in
the Highlands too; perhaps it comes from the union of hill and
river and pasture, failing if one of these is lacking.

One part of the road was barred by a gate. To the old woman
who opened it Dorothy said:

"You live in a very pretty place."
"Yes," said the old woman. "The water of Tweed is a bonny water."

Sometimes they came upon woods, sometimes found "as lovely
a combination of forms as any traveller who goes in search of the
picturesque need desire, and yet perhaps without a single tree"
There was neither barrenness nor rigidity:

"The lines of the hills are flowing and beautiful, the reaches of
the vale long." It was almost a solitude:

"The loneliness of the scattered dwellings . . . aided the general
effect of the gently varying scenes, which was that of tender
pensiveness." This note recurs in Dorothy's account, and it is still
the impression of that valley.

"The murmuring of the river was heard distinctly, often blended with the bleating of sheep." They passed a shepherd, lying on
a sunny slope, his face upturned to the sky: "a happy picture of
shepherd life".

They passed Traquair, low set in the valley, "the hills above it
covered with gloomy fir plantations", the house itself gloomy of
aspect:

"There was an allegorical air in this uncheerful spot, single in
such a country."

Traquair claims to be the oldest inhabited house in Scotland.
Once it belonged to the Stuart Earls of Traquair. The family were
Catholic which still meant a certain seclusion and apartness; they
had been Jacobite in the Forty-five, and the great gates, with the
Bear of their shield and coat-of-arms above them, had been closed
for many a year, to remain so, it was said, until a Stuart king should
come to the throne. Another story (given to the present author
by Scott's great-great-grandson, the late Sir Walter Maxwell-
Scott) is that the Jacobite Earl closed the gates and the avenue
down which he used to drive his coach, because of information

laid against him. In those days, before the passing of the Catholic Emancipation Act, no Catholic might own carriage and horses. Many did, so long as no malignant neighbour informed on them. Lord Traquair was unlucky; an informer told, action had to be taken, his carriage and horses must be given up; in contemptuous wrath he closed the gates. This, however, was not known to William and Dorothy as they stood looking down on the melancholy mansion; nor did they foresee, any more than Scott himself did, that the marriage of one of his descendants and another marriage in the Traquair family would in the present century make the Maxwell-Stuarts of Traquair cousins to the Maxwell-Scotts of Abbotsford.

But to return to that Sabbath day's journey by Tweedside, the Wordsworths came at last to the inn at Clovenford where Scott often stayed on his legal progress, having as yet no house of his own nearer than Lasswade. The Wordsworths mentioned his name and "the woman of the house showed us all possible civility" though she was slow in her ways, unaccustomed to guests. She called Scott "a very clever gentleman". Dorothy adds:

"Mr. Scott is respected everywhere. I believe that by favour of his name one might be hospitably entertained throughout all the Borders of Scotland."

Wordsworth's impression of Tweed between Peebles and Clovenford was of a scene

> More pensive in sunlight
> Than others in moonlight.

They talked of going on to Yarrow but decided instead to make for Melrose. And so Wordsworth came to write a unique poem, not in praise of a place seen and loved but of one unseen and imagined; his "Yarrow Unvisited":

> There's Gala Water, Leader Haughs
>   Both lying right before us;
> And Dryburgh, here with chiming Tweed
>   The lintwhite sing in chorus.
>
> There's pleasant Teviotdale, a land
>   Made blythe with plough and harrow.
> Why throw away a needful day
>   To go in search of Yarrow? . . .

     . . . The swan on still Saint Mary's Lake
       Float double, swan and shadow . . .
     . . . Should life be dull, and spirits low,
       'Twill soothe us in our sorrow
     That earth hath something yet to show—
       The bonny holms of Yarrow.

So they went on to Galashiels—"a pretty place it once has been, but a manufactory is established there; and a townish bustle and ugly stone houses are fast taking the place of the brown-roofed thatched cottages of which a great number still remain, partly overshadowed by trees".

Across the river lay Melrose, and there they met Scott who took them to the Abbey.

"He was here on his own ground," taking them into the heart of it, showing them, and few had more seeing eyes than Dorothy, the almost hidden beauties, the nearly lost glories. Dorothy noted the perfection of the carven leaves and flowers, but also the dismal surroundings; and "surely this is a national barbarism; within these beautiful walls is the ugliest church that was ever beheld—if it had been cut out of the side of a hill, it could not have been more dismal".

The minister at this time was one George Thomson who had a son, also named George, a most learned man whom some claim as the prototype of Dominie Sampson.

They dined with Scott at the inn where they stayed over-night. The respect paid to him, both in his office as Sheriff and in his personality was transmitted to the Wordsworths as his friends, "though I could not persuade the woman to show me the beds, or to make any sort of promise till she was assured from the Sheriff himself that he had no objection to sleep in the same room as William". Next morning he was off early to Jedburgh, the Wordsworths following more leisurely by Dryburgh and Kelso. They liked the landscape here a little less, "the peculiar and pensive simplicity was wanting" although "there was a fertility chequered with wildness" which to some eyes would be ample compensation. They had hoped to breakfast at Dryburgh—had they left Melrose fasting, or was this a second breakfast, luncheon, nuncheon or brunch?—but there was no inn. However, a courteous and hospitable woman invited them into her cottage, into a parlour which impressed Dorothy by the gentility of its furnishing. Her hostess, she discovered, had been maid to Lady Buchan—Lord Buchan was the owner of the Abbey and its grounds—and so had the refinement "a noticeable urbanity" of manner derived from her training and background.

They were admitted to the Abbey by a figure from fairy-tale: a little old woman, bent almost double, with shaggy eyebrows, hooked nose, complexion brown and unwashed, smelling of peat smoke: "If she had emitted smoke by her breath and through every pore, the odour could not have been stronger". But she was a civil guide. Dryburgh was not only a ruin, like Melrose; it had been adapted to the pleasure of the owner who had built a pigeon house, and a fine room where he had held a ball! It was, none the less "a very sweet ruin" set so beautifully among trees which its towers overtopped as in some picture of fairy-tale. And that is still the magic of Dryburgh. No lovelier than its sister abbeys, it surpasses them in its setting of green lawns and cincturing trees.

Having decided to leave Kelso, like Yarrow, unvisited, the Wordsworths went on to Jedburgh, where again they walked in the sunlight of Scott's popularity. The inn was full, taken up by the county Judge and his court, but Dorothy was allowed the use of his sitting-room until the court should rise; and comfortable lodgings were found for them in a neighbouring house with a kind, brisk old woman who insisted on showing Dorothy every corner and cupboard, even opening drawers to display her stock of linen. Meals were sent over from the inn. Wordsworth wrote a poem about their hostess.

Scott came to sit with them and recite part of his *Lay of the Last Minstrel*. They went walking up Jed Water, called at the manse on that most delightful of diarists and historians, Dr. Somerville, attended the Assizes, finding the judge's summing up "the most curious mixture of old woman's oratory and newspaper-paragraph loyalty that ever was heard".

Their hostess was sorry to part with them, telling Dorothy she had behaved "very discreetly" and giving her some of the famous Jeddart pears—a tree still grows there that was bearing fruit when Mary Queen of Scots lay sick almost to death in the town; she was afterwards to wish, poor lady, that she had died at Jeddart. Scott travelled with them into Teviotdale, as far as Hawick where they parted, wishing they could have gone further with him into the countryside "where in almost every house he can find a home and a hearty welcome". Their last sight of his country was from a hill outside Hawick whence they could see the range of Border hills: Carter Fell, Rubislaw, the Cheviots.

By this time Scott was feeling the need of a home in his shrieve-dom. He had not far to seek. A cousin's house, Ashestiel, on Tweedside, fell vacant, its young owner being in India on military service. Scott took it on lease, this old house, "half farm, half manor" as John Buchan describes it, with some pasture land on which he began sheep-rearing in a small way, and with a fine old formal garden. The place was secluded yet not too far from Selkirk or from Edinburgh. "A decent farmhouse overhanging the Tweed, and situated in wild pastoral country" was Scott's own description of it.

Writing to a friend with apologies for not having answered a letter sooner, he explained: "Long sheep and short sheep and tups and gimmers and hogs and dinmonts had made a perfect sheep-fold of my understanding". (Hogs are the young sheep between lambhood and first shearing; they become gimmers when, at a year or a year and a half old they enter the breeding stock; a dinmont is a wether between first and second shearing. The name was to be bestowed upon that sound character Dandie Dinmont, and in turn upon his Border terriers, a breed still flourishing.) As for long and short sheep, the Cheviots were known as long, the original black-faced breed as short. There is a pleasant story of Scott in a company of sheep-farmers whose talk was all of long and short sheep. He pretended to think that the adjectives referred to size of body and asked solemnly:

"How long must a sheep actually measure to come under the denomination of a long sheep?"

"It's the woo', sir, it's the woo' that make's the difference," seriously explained one farmer. "The lang sheep ha'e the short woo', and the short sheep ha'e the long thing, and these are just kind o' names we gi'e them like."

Short sheep or long, they possessed most of the land, and Scott took readily to his new status.

"We are seven miles from kirk and market," he wrote to his friend Ellis. "We rectify the last inconvenience by killing our own mutton and poultry; and as to the former, finding there was some chance of my family turning pagans, I have adopted the goodly practice of reading prayers every Sunday, to the great edification

of my household." Lockhart describes Ashestiel as a perfect home
for a poet; one came to the house through the old-fashioned garden with its green terraced walks and holly hedges. Beneath the
windows was a deep ravine through which ran a mountain stream
on its way to Tweed, and Tweed itself was only the breadth of a
meadow away. All around stood the green hills; Yarrow was
within riding distance "The aspect in every direction is that of
perfect pastoral repose".

Sheep must have a shepherd and one was found who was to
become Scott's faithful servant and friend until death: Tam Purdie.
That worthy had appeared before the Sheriff on a charge of poaching to which he pleaded guilty, but with extenuating circumstances: poverty, a wife and a string of hungry children to feed,
"work scarce and grouse abundant". He made his plea with such
effective pathos and humour that Scott not only forebore impos-
ing a hard sentence, but took Tam into his own employment, first
as shepherd, then, as he proved his worth, as manager of the
sheep-farm. About the same time he took Tam's brother-in-law
Peter Matheson as coachman, to be served with the same fidelity
and devotion. Ashestiel saw the beginning of what was to be a
community under Scott's paternal headship.

"In point of society, according to the heartfelt phrase of Scrip-
ture, we dwelt 'among our own people' ", so Scott wrote many
years later in his introduction to the 1830 edition of *Marmion*.

Friends came to stay. Skene of Rubislaw came in the August of
1805. "You know the way, and the ford is where it was, which,
by the way, is more than I expected," Scott wrote to him. There
had been a thunder-storm with floods of rain. Skene duly arrived
and has left a record of his visit and of Scott's way of life which
would not be greatly altered over the years, at Ashestiel or at
Abbotsford. His days were full; for most men literature or the
law alone would have been enough and he was deep in both,
besides his activity as a countryman. He used to rise early, about
five o'clock, light his fire, dress and shave carefully, for he detested slovenly "bed-gown and slipper tricks", then settle to writing for three hours, until breakfast, so being able "to break the
neck of the day's work". After breakfast he returned to his desk
for two hours more or so, but by noon or by one o'clock at latest,
he was "his own man" or his guests' man, ready to ride out with
them.

Children and dogs enlivened the house: Camp, the serious dog, his favourite, with whom he talked as man to man, Douglas and Percy the frivolous young greyhounds. Host and guest rode over the hills, coursed a hare, speared salmon in Tweed—this, for preference, by night, with torches, "burning the water". It was not, by Skene's account, easy sport; the salmon lay in the depths, not quickly to be discerned, and the fisherman thrusting hopefully might find that his eyes had deceived him, and be plunged into the pool himself, losing fish and spear and torch. Scott took one header like this, and was rescued only by Skene's clutch at his coat. Those were the risks; "the pleasures consisted in being penetrated with cold and wet, having your shins broken against the stones in the dark, and perhaps mastering one fish out of every twenty you take aim at".

For all that, the sport continued; fishermen would appear to be impervious to wet, to be akin to mermen. Tweedside breeds a hardy race and hardens those it attracts from other parts. Fishing and salmon spearing were not the only ploys. They went riding through Ettrick and Yarrow, into the little glens, up among the hills. There was always a royal welcome for Scott, for this was his kingdom, and no king was ever more secure of allegiance. They rode and walked and rested, Skene with his sketch-book while Scott sat by him, reciting a ballad, telling an old tale, talking of the folk they met. A few years later in 1808 Scott published *Marmion*. This is not the place to discuss his poetry, but one peculiar charm must be noted: his Introductions to each Canto, each being an epistle in verse to a friend, descriptive, evocative of the setting, recalling shared experiences, sometimes talking of contemporary events. Canto Four begins with an address to Skene, written in November, when the gale

> Whirls the dry leaves on Yarrow's shore . . .
> And Blackhouse heights and Ettrick Pen
> Have donned their wintry shrouds again

He recalls their summer wanderings: "thou with pencil, I with pen" and the shepherd who

> outstretched the livelong day,
> At ease among the heath-flowers lay,
> Viewed the light clouds with vacant look,
> Or slumbered o'er his tattered book,

> Or idly busied him to guide
> His angle o'er the lessen'd tide.

Dorothy Wordsworth had seen a shepherd thus take his ease. But she had not seen him as Scott did, in winter, wrapping himself in his plaid, calling his reluctant dogs from the hearth, and going out into the drifting snow to rescue his flock:

> If fails his heart, if his limbs fail,
> Benumbing death is in the gale;
> His paths, his landmarks all unknown
> Close to the hut, no more his own.

So it could happen in any night of storm; so it has happened many a winter since; it happened in the long snow of 1963.

Marmion was begun one winter, continued in the next. The first Canto is addressed to William Stewart Rose.

> November's sky is chill and drear,
> November's leaf is red and sear;
> Late, gazing down the steepy linn
> That hems our little garden in,
>
> Low in its dark and narrow glen,
> You scarce the rivulet might ken . . .
> An angry brook, it sweeps the glade,
> Brawls over rock and wild cascade,
> And, foaming brown with doubled speed,
> Hurries its waters to the Tweed.

The purple and crimson of autumn were gone with the heather

> That bloomed so rich on Neidpath fell;
> Sallow his brow; and russet bare
> Are now the sister heights of air.

The sheep were driven to the valleys for shelter and herbage, the dogs follow their master dejectedly, dreading the mounting gale. Scott's children were despondent.

> My imps, though hardy, bold and wild,
> As best befits the mountain child,
> Feel the sad influence of the hour,
> And wail the daisys vanished flower.

demanding whether spring will ever return. Yet they were luckier than most bairns. They had a father who could tell them tales and ballads.

Even on those summer and autumn days there could be menace. Skene recalls one adventure in the hills above Moffat, looking down on Loch Skene and the cascade of The Grey Mare's Tail. They were lost in the mist and bogged in a peat-slough; fortunately they were riding hill ponies that could extricate themselves and so, unhurt though miry, they came to the dark loch, while an eagle rose, screaming in his flight:

"It would be impossible to picture anything more desolately savage than the scene which opened, as if raised by enchantment to gratify the poet's eye; thick folds of fog rolling incessantly over the face of the inky waters, but rent asunder now in one direction, then in another—so as to afford us a glimpse of some projecting rock or naked point of land or island bearing a few scraggy stumps of pine, and then closing again in universal darkness upon the cheerless waste."

It is a far cry from the pensive tranquillity of landscape which delighted the Wordsworths; but both pictures are true, both aspects are part of the Scott country; as tranquillity and horror are both part of Scott's genius and creation. There was a dark side to his imagination, revealed in flashes of poetry, in scraps of dialogue, in a phrase, an incident, as well as the great geniality we chiefly associate with him.

Skene's graphic talent was not confined to his pencil. A modern reader may find in that description something resembling passages in Tolkien's *Lord of the Rings*. Frodo and his companions might have come to such a region.

Skene tells us that some of the scenery for *Old Mortality* was taken from that ride; and on this expedition they met an odd creature, "one of those itinerants who gain a subsistance among the moorland farmers by relieving them of foxes, polecats and the like", known locally as Tod (or Fox) Willie, immortalised as Tod Gabbie in *Guy Mannering*.

Some years were to pass before The Great Unknown captivated the imagination of Europe with his novels, but the seed lay in his mind long before he set pen to paper. He carried with him a store of remembered pictures, phrases, characters. C. S. Lewis has said that the genesisi of his Narnia stories was a picture, or a series of pictures, clear in his mind. How much of Scott's creation began thus has not been recorded or estimated but it may be guessed: the landscape, peaceful or terrible, the odd character, the vivid phrase, the scrap of story. Only the creator himself, and not always he can tell how they grow and merge into the work of art.

There were other days, more tranquil: in Yarrow at St. Mary's Loch, at other places whose very names make poetry: "The Teviot and the Alt, Borthwick Water and the lonely towers of Buccleuch and Harden, Minto, Roxburgh, Gilnockie."

They went by Borthwick to Langholm, to stay with Lord and Lady Dalkeith, "upon which occasion the otter-hunt so well described in *Guy Mannering* was got up by our noble host", much to Scott's delight. They followed all the rivers of the Borders but Tweed was first and dearest, known from source to mouth, in every valley, by stream and ford: "He had an amazing fondness for fords", preferring them to bridges, although his lameness must have hampered him on stepping stones. Once, fording Ettrick, he remembered a story about a water kelpie and must stop to tell it, which he did with such animation that he lost his foothold, slipped and took a ducking; or it may be that the kelpie clutched him.

Scott was in his prime then, a man in the thirties, not yet near the height of his fame and fortune but, one might say, on the pleasant foothills. Well thought of as Sheriff he had that other delectable reputation as a poet; but he wanted more. He would be a laird. Ashestiel may have kindled this delight in possession, "yird-hunger" or passion for land which was to dominate his life as love of women has dominated other men. If he had been able to buy Ashestiel it might have satisfied him; it was not for sale, however, his cousin wanted to retain it, and when his lease was up Scott must look about for another home. He had money in hand from the sale of the house in Kelso, Rosebank, left him by his uncle Robert Scott. He remembered something his father had once shown him as they drove along Tweed from Selkirk to Melrose.

"We must get out here, Walter," the elder Scott had said, "and see something quite in your line."

This was a stone on the bank half a mile above the river, marking the site of the Battle of Melrose, in 1526, between Homes, Kerrs and the Earl of Angus on one side, Buccleugh and his Scotts on the other, for possession of the person of the young King James V. At this point, since called Turn-Again, the victorious Scotts had turned back from the pursuit of the Kerrs.

It might have been called Return-Again for Scott was captivated and came back, and when he wanted a place of his own he
remembered it. The land and small farm were for sale; they belonged to the minister of Galashiels, Dr. Douglas who, as a young
man had been the friend and correspondent of Mrs. Cockburn,
born Rutherford, author of one version of "The Flowers O' the
Forest" (of whom more will be told). The property was called
Carleyhole, but from its condition was generally known as
Clartyhole (or Dirtyhole) a poor place, without dykes or drainage; but Scott fell in love with it as a man might with a plain
woman in whom he sees a charm and grace hidden from other
eyes. He bought it from Dr. Douglas in 1811, and so began his
love affair with "that Delilah" as Sir Herbert Grierson has called
Abbotsford, the house and estate which seduced him into extrava-
glance. Scott was a faithful and devoted husband—but Abbotsford
was his mistress.

In 1812 he brought his family to their new home, still far from
finished. The Making of Abbotsford, as his great-granddaughter
was to call it, continued for many years, as Clartyhole threw off
its nickname and emerged out of dreariness and shabbiness into
comfort, gentility, even grandeur.

The children, Sophia, Walter, Anne and Charles were respectively thirteen, eleven, nine and seven years of age. They
would be young grown-ups by the time Abbotsford was
finished.

Meanwhile—"Our flitting and removal from Ashestiel baffled
all description", Scott wrote to his friend Daniel Terry, the actor,
in London. "We had twenty-four cart-loads of the veriest trash
in nature, besides dogs, pigs, poneys, poultry, cows, calves, bare-
headed wenches and bare-breeched boys." One of the dogs was
missing: Percy the greyhound had died, and was buried under
a stone inscribed, for the bewilderment of future antiquarians: "Ci
gist le preux Percie". Many faithful dogs lie in their little burial
corner at Abbotsford above the river.

These first months were something of a picnic. The family
stayed at Abbotsford as Scott re-named the place, while he himself spent the week in Edinburgh attending the Court of Session;
he used to appear on Saturday morning wearing country clothes
under his gown, ready to be off to the Borders as soon as the Court
rose. His vacations were spent there, in much activity and little

Ashiestiel House
Scott's wine cooler in the grounds of Chiefswood House

quiet. One room had to serve as family sitting-room, dining-room, school-room and study; the writing table in the window, which could be curtained off from the rest of the room marked Scott's domain. He wrote as Jane Austen did in the thick of family life, tolerant of interruptions. He was writing his poem *Rokeby*, hammering at it, he said, while the masons hammered at the new walls. His muse was imperturbable, undistressed by "the surrounding confusion of masons and carpenters, to say nothing of the lady's small talk, the children's babble".

Sometimes he laid aside pen for chisel, to have a share in the building, or for a spade to plant trees for future generations to enjoy. It was his resolve, he told Byron, whom he had met in London, at John Murray's, to make a silk purse out of a sow's ear.

Abbotsford was gradually made, or one might say it grew; and it is the sense of growth about it that makes it unique, that redeems it from the faults a purist in architecture might deplore. Scott's first plan was for a large "cottage orné" in the style then in vogue among the romantic, or a house in the style of an English vicarage, not a mansion but ample enough to be a family house in the widest sense:

"I cannot relinquish my Border principle of accommodating all the cousins and duniwastles who will rather sleep on chairs and on the floor, and in the lay-loft, than be absent when folks are gathered together."

Mrs. Scott was a good housewife and she was houseproud. The rooms at first might be few and small but they had charm. Skene came on a visit once, just before Scott's return from a journey to Paris, and found his hostess and her daughters happy in their little drawing-room which was "fitted up with new chintz furniture". They looked forward to Scott's surprise and pleasure. He arrived, his pleasure in being home again was obvious—but he took no notice of the new chintzes until his wife's patience gave out, and she demanded the praise she deserved. It was then given in full measure.

"Abbotsford begins this season to look the whimsical, gay old cabin that we had chalked out," he reported in 1814. "I have made the old farm-house my *corps de logis* with some outlying places for kitchen, laundry, and two spare bedrooms."

Two years later were added "a handsome boudoir" opening into the little drawing-room "to which it serves as chapel-of-ease";

The sweep of the River Tweed, looking across to the Eildons

by 1820 there was a new, large drawing-room for his wife, hung
with Chinese wall-paper in soft green, patterned with exotic birds
and foliage, which is, through the mellowing of time, perhaps
even more charming today than when it first delighted its owners.
There was "a handsome library", the long room lined with books,
with its great bay-window looking down on Tweed. Next to
this was his study, also book-lined, small, a true writer's work-
shop. Its most delightful feature is the little stair in one corner,
leading up to the gallery which runs round the room about two-
thirds of the height up. In a corner of the gallery is a door leading
to Scott's dressing-room. He kept up that habit of early rising,
coming down to his study to work before breakfast, then join
family and guests in the big dining-room which also looks upon
Tweed; breakfast often of wheaten bread and kippered salmon,
before the activity of the day.

His poems continued, his novels were begun. From Abbotsford
in 1814, from "the whimsical, gay old cabin" the manuscript of
Waverley was sent to the publishers, and fame followed with a
rush. Scott the Sheriff, the Laird ("We are not a little proud of
being greeted as Laird and Lady") became also The Great Unknown. It is characteristic of the man that this became his family
nickname.

As the cottage grew into a mansion, so the few fields became an
estate. Scott was hungry for land, to have and to hold as his own,
to leave to the family he saw himself founding, of Scott of Abbotsford. Gradually he bought other small estates, Kaeside, Chiefswood, Huntlyburn—originally called Toftfield, which he let to
his friend Adam Fergusson. The new name was given at the
request of the ladies of the family, from the burn that ran through
the grounds, the burn on whose bank Thomas the Rhymer was
lying when he encountered the Fairy Queen and her company,
and went with them to Elfland. The Rhymer's Glen became part
of Scott's domain.

It was not until 1825 that he could write proudly: "Abbotsford
is now all that I can makę it." Long before then, however, it was
a comfortable, hospitable and much-loved home. The garden
grew with the house; a square court lay outside the front door,
and beyond it, separated by a stone screen, was the garden.

While the house was still a-building there was a party, reported
by Lockhart years later, with loving recollection. In October 1818

he, a young advocate and man of letters of some promise, was bidden, with his friend John Wilson and one or two others, to stay with the man he had begun greatly to like and admire. Scott took them up to one of the towers, looking across to Galashiels. Downstairs, the dining-room was unfinished but capable of holding the company. Scott's piper, John Bruce, John of Skye, struck up a tune and they danced to his piping, danced until they nearly wore out the soles of their shoes, as the phrase goes in some of the old tales. The house was lit by the new, exciting gas, the first in Scotland to be so illumined; and by gas it continued to be lit until 1962 when electricity was conveyed to it.

When they were weary of dancing, refreshments were brought in, and Lord Melville proposed a toast to the roof-tree.

"Such was the *handsel*, for Scott protested against its being considered the *house-heating* of the new Abbotsford."

Sophia was then nineteen, a girl of much comeliness if not actual beauty, and great charm and kindliness; she was a sweet singer, delighting her father with the old Scots songs he loved, to the accompaniment of the harp—which still stands in the drawing-room. She had much of her father in her, his warmth and kindliness, and wisdom. Lockhart fell in love, she was not unresponsive (her first letter to him is treasured at Abbotsford). About a year and a half after this visit, in April 1820, they were married, and set up house in Great King Street, Edinburgh. Scott gave them Chiefswood for a country home and it became his own favourite escape from the throng of visitors at Abbotsford. By the time of this marriage he had become Sir Walter Scott of Abbotsford, one of the most famous men in Scotland and beyond, one of the best loved in his own Border country.

The rest may be briefly told. This marriage was deeply happy, shadowed only by the delicacy and early death of their first-born, Scott's adored grandson John Hugh, for whom he wrote his *Tales of a Grandfather*. There were two other children, Walter and Charlotte. The shadows fell again more darkly when Sophia died at only thirty-seven. None of Scott's children had long life; Anne, who after her mother's death, nursed him devotedly through his last long illness, died only nine months later, worn out; Charles, his younger son, a man of much charm and talent died at thirty-five; Walter, the soldier alone of the four lived into his forties. He married but had no children.

Young Walter Lockhart thus became heir to Abbotsford; on his death, sadly young, Charlotte succeeded. She had married James Hope, a cadet of the family of the Earl of Hopetoun (now Marquis of Linlithgow) and they assumed the name of Hope-Scott. They were among those devout Anglicans who, turned towards Catholic tradition by the Oxford Movement, entered the Roman Catholic Church, along with Hope-Scott's friend, Henry Manning the future Cardinal. Catholic life on the Borders owed much to their zeal.

Hope-Scott, a Parliamentary lawyer, was wealthy, and like many Victorians chose to put much of his wealth into stone and lime—or did Abbotsford again compel tribute? The house was already a place of pilgrimage for tourists, and some privacy was needed. He built a new entrance on the farther side of the court from the garden; to the left of the door was his study with a chapel beyond it where Newman, when he stayed at Abbotsford, celebrated Mass. On the right a long corridor led to a large sitting-room with a garden door on to the court, a book-room, and beyond that the morning-room and dining-room of Scott's own house. Upstairs more bedrooms were added. Victorian and Catholic Abbotsford was grafted into the house Scott had made; another layer of atmosphere was added, almost another dimension. The personality of the house was not diminished.

Charlotte unhappily inherited and transmitted her mother's delicacy. Only one of her children survived her and lived to maturity, a daughter, Mary Monica usually called Mamo. She married the Hon. Joseph Constable-Maxwell, son of Lord Herries, of an old Galloway family, and they assumed the surname of Maxwell-Scott. Their eldest son Walter succeeded his mother as Laird of Abbotsford; in 1932, the centenary of Scott's death, the extinct baronetage was revived in his favour. Today his daughters, Patricia and Jean, great-great-great-granddaughters of Sir Walter Scott, live in this beloved home.

The historic rooms created and used by Scott, the hall and armoury, library and study, drawing-room and dining-room are open to the public from March to October. But this is very far from being merely a museum or a half-empty house. These rooms are part of a living home; to pass from these rooms into the private family part is to walk through time, and find the barriers almost impalpable. This is still Scott's home, in the heart of his own country; his benign presence is here. He liked people; those who come here, as guests or as tourists, are aware of a welcome.

A Portrait of the Scott Country must survey both past and present. It must not be forgotten that Scott, the lover of ballads and old tales, the antiquarian, the historical, romantic novelist, was also a man of his times, a man of affairs, alert to contemporary matters. He wrote about the current affairs and problems of Scotland, he made the Borders known, and helped to renew their life for the future.

Something will be said in a later chapter about tweed, the great manufacture of the Border towns; Scott helped to make it fashionable as he made ballads and narrative verse fashionable. He was the last man to think himself or be thought by others a dandy or a man of fashion; but he was famous, and when he appeared in London wearing trousers of shepherd's plaid or black-and-white-checked tweed he set a vogue which still continues. The variety of tweeds today in colour and pattern is beyond any nineteenth-century weaver's dream. The great weaver of tales had his part in beginning its progress towards fame and fashion.

II

BACKGROUND OF HISTORY AND LEGEND

From the remote period when the Roman province was contracted by the ramparts of Severus, until the Union of the Kingdoms, the Borders of Scotland formed the stage upon which were presented the most memorable conflicts of two gallant nations.

—Scott: Introduction to *The Border Minstrelsy*

The inhabitants, living in a state partly pastoral and partly warlike, and combining habits of constant depredation with the influence of a rude spirit of chivalry, were often engaged in scenes highly suscep-tive of poetical ornament.

—Scott, Introduction to *The Lay of the Last Minstrel*

GEOGRAPHICALLY the Scott Country is marchland, debatable, lying on the brink of England; it is marchland and debatable, too, in its division between great families once prone to strife: Scott, Kerr, Douglas and the rest. Historically and metaphorically it lies on the borders between authentic, written records and legend, in a shadowy realm where anything may have happened, where credulity may often be the best guide. Strangeness is no contra-diction of truth and fact.

The Borders saw the coming of the Romans, the building of Hadrian's Wall across Northumberland and Cumberland, of Antonine's between Forth and Clyde. Sir George Douglas has called Tacitus' *Agricola*, that early masterpiece of biography, "the false dawn of Border history" in which the light of literature shines briefly on the scene, before a thousand years of darkness.

But were they so dark? There are still gleams of light shining through what is a mist rather than thick darkness.

This is part of Roman Britain. At Newstead in Roxburgh there was a Roman camp, Trimontium; there are remains of forts at Torwoodlee, and at Oakwood near Selkirk. Many fragments of

Roman glass and pottery have been found. There are other forts too; the circular brochs built, some think, by raiders from the north, others say by the native Cymri or British in defence against the Picts, the Angles and the Saxons. There is above all the Catrail which, as one local historian has said, "almost halves Selkirkshire in two", that great fosse or ditch or dyke, fifty miles long, running through Selkirk and Roxburgh to Peel Fell in the Cheviots, from Torwoodlee, past a camp at Rinkhill, on to Tweed and Yair and into Berwickshire, Scott once tried to jump his horse across it, on Scott of Gala's land; he was thrown and badly bruised and shaken. Andrew Lang makes it the place of treasure-trove in his story *The Gold of Fairnilee*—of which more hereafter.

There are Standing Stones on Hownam Steeple, known as the Shearers and the Bandsters which, according to Sir George Douglas, may have begun a local legend of judgement upon Sabbath-workers and Sabbath-breakers.

With the departure of the Romans came not peace but warfare between native British and invading tribes of Picts, of Angles and Saxons. The mist becomes faintly gold with the light of legend glimmering through; into this shadowy borderland of history King Arthur comes riding, not, at first sight, the Arthur of Camelot and the Round Table, of the Quest for the Grail, but another manifestation of him, of the hero who comes to defend his people. In this Border tradition he leads the British against their foes from north and west, against Hengist and his hordes from the south. The battleground lay in this Border country and here Arthur fought his twelve great battles to set Britain free, to defend Christianity against the old paganism; he fought against the traitor Modred. One was fought at Coit Celidon or Wood of Celidon in the Forest of Ettrick, one at Castle Guinnion in Wedale or Gala Valley. Arthur was victorious, but he was slain; or, some say, carried away, hurt but living, not to Avalon but within the Eildon hill where he and his knights still sleep, armed and ready, their horses stabled near them, to waken and ride out at a summons in Britain's ultimate need.

Inseparable from Arthur in every form or variant of the legend is Merlin the enchanter. Was there one Merlin or were there two? He was certainly one of the Bards of Britain—Aneurin and Taliessin being others, and to poets and bards the legend of magic was often attached, as it was, in the Middle Ages, to Virgil. Merlin too comes to us out of that golden mist which lies between the darkness of oblivion and the daylight of history. As Arthur personifies the eternal hero, deliverer and champion, so Merlin is the incarnation of wizardry, the poet-mage, the spell-binder and magic-worker.

In this Border tradition he is no friend to Arthur but his foe, the last of the pagans. It is said that after the last battle he wandered about Tweeddale, fugitive and masterless, that, becoming crazed in his wits he was mocked and dreaded by the people, finally set upon and stoned to death by shepherds, panic-stricken by fear of what power might still be in him, infected it may be by his fear of them. His grave, by this tradition, is by the Powsail Burn near Drummelzier Kirk.

A kindlier story tells of his meeting St. Kentigern or Mungo the beloved Bishop and Saint of Strathclyde, of being converted to the Christian faith and dying a christened man. Yet another legend sends him not to the grave but into Eildon, to sit with Arthur and his knights in enchanted slumber; so he too may come again.

If all this be not true it is yet well found, and credible by all men gifted with perception and imagination. In all legend and tradition there is at least a sub-stratum of truth.

Merlin has spiritual descendants in this country of poetry and magic. First of them is Thomas the Rhymer, Thomas Learmont, to give him his real surname, Thomas of Ercildoune or Earlston on the Leader. He was a real person, a real poet, a real Border laird, in the thirteenth century, the reputed author of *The Romance of Tristram*. So much is recorded; what is further told and believed is that he left this earth for Elfhame for seven long years:

> True Thomas lay on Huntlie Bank,
> A ferlie he spied wi' his e'e.

The ferlie or marvel was no less than the Fairy Queen herself with all her company. Thomas, like Bottom, was translated but his adventures were not comic. For seven years he dwelt with the Fairy Queen, doing her service, learning many things. When he came again to Ercildoune he had a strange new wisdom; his was the tongue "that will never lee", and he was known thenceforth as True Thomas. His prophecies were fulfilled. The best known concerns the Haigs of Bemersyde:

> Tyde what may betyde,
> Haig shall be laird of Bemersyde.

He foretold the death of Alexander III, by which the crown of Scotland passed to his granddaughter the Maid of Norway; she, being drowned on her way to her kingdom left Scotland torn between rival claimants to the throne, and hence came much woe. He foretold the tragedy of Flodden and the fate of James IV who like Arthur, seemed to fall in battle but was believed by many to have been carried away from the field, wounded but alive, to some place of refuge and healing:

> Out of the field he shall be led,
> When he is bludie and woe for blude;
>
> Yet to his men shall he say
> "For God's love turn you again,
> And give yon suthern folk a frey! [fright]
> Why should I lose the right is mine,
> My fate is not to die this day".

A modern historian and teller of tales, the late William Croft Dickinson, made delightful use of this legend in his story "The Flag of The Isles" in which two children of today, translated by magic into the past, go with the King and his escort and see him carried over the sea to Skye and to safety.

He told of the Union of the Crowns:

> A French queene shall bear the sonne
>   Shall rule all Britain to the sea;
> Which of the Bruce's blood shall come,
>   As near as the ninth degree.

But this Scott held to be a forgery written after the event. A very practical forecast ran:

> At Eildon Tree if you shall be,
> A bridge o'er Tweed ye there shall see.

Scott commented: "In fact, you may now see no less than three bridges."

The Ballad of Thomas the Rhymer is one of the most magic that human tongue has recited or human ear heard:

It was mirk, mirk nicht, and there was nae stern licht,
And they waded through red blude to the knee;
For a' the blude that's shed on earth
    Rins through the streams o' that countrie . . .

Syne they cam' to a garden green,
    And she pu'ed an aipple frae a tree:
"Tak' that for thy wages, True Thomas,
    It will give thee the tongue that can never lee' . . .
. . . "He's gotten a coat of the even cloth,
    And a pair of shoon o' the velvet green;
And till seven years were gane and past,
    True Thomas on earth was never seen".

And even then his return was but for a time. Of his own fate he predicted:

The hare shall kittle [litter] on my hearth stane,
And there will never be a Laird Learmont again.

So it came to pass. In *The Border Minstrelsy* Scott adds his own ballad of the sequel. When Thomas's appointed time was near its end

The feast was spread in Ercildoune,
In Learmont's high and ancient hall,

where Thomas entertained his guests with harping and the chanted tale of King Arthur, and Tristram and Isolde, so that the ladies wept and the lords

Half ashamed, the rugged cheek
Did many a gauntlet dry.

That night, one of them, Lord Douglas, lay wakeful. Hearing footsteps he went out, and in the moonlight he saw a hart and hind that had left the forest and come pacing through the hamlet to the hall itself. Thomas came out, his harp slung round his neck, to follow them, turning to bid farewell to Ercildoune:

And Leader's wave, like silver sheen
    Danced shimmering in the ray;
In deepening mass, at distance seen,
    Dark Soltra's mountains lay.

"Farewell, my father's ancient tower,
   A long farewell", said he;
... "Farewell to Leader's silver tide,
   Farewell to Ercildoune".

... Some said to hill, and some to glen,
   Their wondrous course had been;
But never in haunts of living men
   Again was Thomas seen.

The legend has been taken up by later writers. Mrs. Craik, who wrote that edifying Victorian best-seller *John Halifax, Gentleman* wrote also some fairy-tales, including that of "Alice Learmont"—about a descendant of True Thomas, taken like him into Elfhame but redeemed by the compulsive love of her mother. And Professor Croft Dickinson in another of his tales for children, the first of three, tells how two children at "The Eildon Tree" met Thomas and were led by him into faery, but not for long, and with a safe return.

Scott has compared his fame as poet-seer with that of Virgil the Wizard. There is one less-known account of him which says he left the world for the religious life in a monastery.

The last of the three legendary soothsayers or wizards is Michael Scott, born, probably in the late twelfth century, probably in Tweeddale; educated at Roxburgh, proceeding to Durham, Oxford and Bologna which was not an unusual scholar's progress in the Middle Ages when colleges and universities were few but were international in membership. He is to be heard of at Palermo about 1200 to 1209 as tutor to the young Frederick II, the future Emperor and *stupor mundi*, and Michael was to astound the world himself. There he learned Greek, which was far less known at the time than Latin, the language of the Church and the common tongue of men of any education, and also Arabic; then he went to Toledo to study chemistry or alchemy, and this, added to his already wide learning, gained him the name of wizard. Returning to Scotland about 1230 he is said to have lived at Melrose and died there, and been buried in the Abbey.

One of the lighter tales of him is that he was troubled by persistent demons; in order to be rid of them he set them three tasks: the first, to split Eildon into three peaks, was quickly done; so was the second which was to bridle Tweed with a cauld or dam.

The third, to make ropes of sand at Tweedmouth keeps them busy still.

Scott, in his *Lay of the Last Minstrel* tells how the knight, William of Deloraine rides from Branksome Tower at the bidding of its Lady who had secret knowledge and secret power, to seek "the Monk of St. Mary's Aisle" and bid him open the tomb of Michael and find his magic book. It is St. Michael's Night, feast of the wizard's patron the archangel, when the heavenly powers are strong.

> Though the stars be dim, the moon is bright,
> And the Cross, of bloody red,
> Will point to the grave of the mighty dead.

Here occurs the vivid and celebrated description of the Abbey by the poet who loved it so well; description both of the present ruin and of the complete loveliness that once had stood there:

> If thou wouldst view fair Melrose aright,
> Go visit it by the pale moonlight;
> For the gay beams of lightsome day
> Gild but to flout the ruins grey . . .
> . . . When buttress and buttress alternately
> Seem form'd of ebon and ivory,
> When silver edges the imagery,
> And the scrolls that teach thee to live and die,
> When the distant Tweed is heard to rave,
> And the owlet to hoot o'er the dead man's grave,
> Then go—but go alone the while—
> Then view St. David's ruined pile;
> And home returning soothly swear
> Was never scene so sad and fair.

It is the new splendour that the knight sees when the Monk leads him through cloister garth and cloisters:

> Spreading herbs and flowerets bright
> Glistened with the dew of night;
> Nor herb nor floweret glistened there
> But was carved in the cloister-arches as fair.

It was this delicate and precise beauty which captivated Dorothy Wordsworth. They come into the church and the chancel with its roof above the "pillars lofty and light and small", the carved keystone and corbels.

> The moon on the western oriel shone
> Through slender shafts of shapely stone,
> By foliaged tracery combined;
> Thou would'st have thought some fairy's hand
> 'Twixt poplars straight the osier band
> In many a freakish knot had twined,
> Then framed a spell when the work was done,
> And changed the willow wreaths to stone.

The moon shines through the blazonry of the window, through the image of St. Michael with his red cross, its light falling blood-red on the pavement. Monk and knight talk by the tomb of Robert the Bruce, the monk recalling his own warrior youth, his meeting in far, pagan lands with Michael Scott who taught him some of his knowledge, including the word of power which cleft Eildon in three and "bridled the Tweed with a curb of stone". He had summoned the young man to his death-bed:

> I was in Spain when the morning rose,
> But I stood by his bed ere evening close

—there to hear words that must not be spoken again:

> They would rend this Abbaye's massy nave,
> And pile it in heaps above his grave,

and to be bidden bury with the Wizard his magic book; never to be revealed

> Save at his Chief of Branksome's need.

So Michael the Wizard was buried on the night of St. Michael the Archangel:

> Where the floor of the chancel was stained red,
> That his patron's cross mught over him wave,
> And scare the fiends from the Wizard's grave.

Now the stone is raised; the knight sees the body of Michael, still uncorrupt, seeming to be seventy years old, wrapped in a pilgrim's coat, holding his book in one hand, a silver cross in the other, a lamp by his knee, a lamp with light streaming out.

> High and majestic was his look
> At which the foulest fiends had shook,
> And all unruffled as his face;
> They trusted his soul had gotten grace.

—And so proceeds the tale, sung by the Minstrel in Newark to the young Duchess of Buccleuch and her ladies; Scott wrote the lay for a future Duchess, the Countess of Dalkeith.

His poem is in the true Border tradition. The ballads are full of magic. These are the oldest of all, older than the historical ballads of war and raid and captivity. They are as old as the hills. Thomas the Rhymer was led into Elfhame; young Tam of the Lin at Carterhaugh had a like fate. He came to earth there, at times, and no maid should go to meet him who wished to keep her maidenhood. Fair Janet went, her yellow hair braided, her green kirtle kilted above her knees. She pulled a rose, and Tam Lin came to her:

> He's taen her by the milk-white hand,
> And by the grass-green sleeve,
> He's led her to the fairy ground,
> At her he asked nae leave.

When she came again to her father's hall it was not for her lost maidenhood she looked so wan and woeful, but because she feared her lover was not of mortal blood.

> "O Tell me, tell me, Tam", she said,
> "For His Sake That died on tree.
> If ever ye were in holy chapel,
> Or sained in Christentie?"

Tam assures her that he is a christened man, held by the Fairy Queen; he dwells in their pleasant land, but once in seven years they must pay teind to hell:

> I am sae fair and fu' o' flesh,
> I fear it be mysel!.

Only Janet can save him, that very night of Hallowe'en; she must await the riding of the fairy host, pull him from his horse, endure all the changes in him, speak no word.

> Aboot the deid hour o' the nicht,
> She heard the bridles ring,

And Janet was as glad o' that,
As ony earthly thing.

She is obedient through every dreadful test, and saves her lover,
to the bitter anger of the Queen:

Had I the wit yestreen, yestreen,
That I hae coft this day [bought]
I'd paid my teind seven times to hell
Ere you had been won away.

The haunting beauty of the ballads lies in their simplicity, their
starkness of phrase. They make a statement—of terror, of grief,
of supernatural fear or mortal heartbreak; that is all.

Love can conquer strong magic; it can endure beyond death
with only faith for company. A girl seeks her lost love by Yarrow
—Willie who was fair and rare and bonny:

"Yestreen I made my bed fu' braid,
The nicht I'll mak' it narrow,
For a' the live-long winter's nicht
I lie twined [bereft] o' my marrow".

She sought him east, she sought him wast,
She sought baith braid and narro;
Syne, in the clifting o' a crag,
She found him drowned in Yarrow.

A lover lingers by his love's grave:

The wind doth blow to-day, my love,
And a few small drops of rain;
I never had but one true love,
In cauld grave she has lain.

He seems to hear her bid him depart. This is realistic grief; if
he kissed her now, her lips would be clay cold, and she would
smell of death. Hearts decay like flowers:

So make yourself content, my love,
Till God calls you away.

Yarrow claimed many a victim. A favourite ballad, as Scott
found, among the people of Ettrick Forest was The Dowie Dens
of Yarrow. It is a tale of enmity and treachery within one clan

—the Scotts, between a Scott of Harden and them of Gilmans-cleugh; a forced fight thrust on one man:

> Late at e'en, drinking the wine,
> And e'er they paid the lawing,
> They set a combat them between
> To fight it on the dawing.

It was no fair fight—nine against one; Harden's wife tries to hold him back, having dreamed an ill-omened dream. When she comes after him, she finds him slain:

> She kissed his cheek, she kaimed his hair,
> She searched his wounds all thorough,
> She kissed them till her lips grew red,
> On the dowie houms of Yarrow.

There is The Douglas Tragedy too, where Lady Margaret escapes with her lover, Lord William, and her father and seven brothers ride in pursuit; Lord William kills them one by one, and she sheds no tear until the end:

> "O, haud your hand, Lord William", she said,
> "For your strokes they are wondrous sair;
> True lovers I can get many an ane,
> But a faither I can never get mair".

And now she must ride on with him, for she has no other guide or protector.

> O, they rade on, and on they rade,
> And a' by the licht o' the moon,
> Until they came to yon wan water,
> And there they lichted doun.

to drink; and as they drink the water is red with Lord William's blood. But he tells her:

> "'Tis naething but the shadow of my scarlet cloak
> That shines in the water sae plain."

On they ride again by the light of the moon, till they come to his mother's house where they are bedded; but:

> Lord William was dead lang ere midnight,
> Lady Margaret lang ere day.

They were buried one in St. Mary's Kirk, one in the choir:

> Out o' the lady's grave grew a bonny red rose,
> And out o' the knight's a brier.

which met and intertwined to show that two lovers slept beneath.
But one day the Black Douglas came riding by:

> And wow, but he was rough!
> For he pu'ed up the bonny brier,
> And flang't in St. Mary's Loch.

Scott adds that this is one of the few ballads given a precise
locality by popular tradition; at the farm of Blackhouse in Selkirkshire once stood a tower, whence Lady Margaret was carried
off by her lover; the Douglas Burn was the wan water that ran
red with blood.

Even without human treachery the rivers could claim their men.

> Said Tweed to Till:
> "What gars ye rin sae still?"
> Said Till to Tweed:
> "Though ye rin wi' speed,
> And I rin slaw,
> For ae man thet ye droun,
> I droun twa."

Jacobite loyalty and Jacobite suffering are hardly part of the
Border story as they are of the Highlands. The Stuart Kings were
no friends to many bold Borderers. The Border Widow laments
her husband, Cockburne of Henderland in Ettrick, one of the
freebooters hanged by James V, over the gate of his own tower.
His servants fled and his widow was left alone: alone she watched
the corpse, and sewed his winding sheet:

> I took his body on my back,
>   And whiles I ga'ed and whiles I sat;
> I digged a grave and laid him in,
>   And happed him wi' the sod sae green.
>
> But think ye na my he'rt was sair,
>   When I laid the moul' on his yellow hair;
> O think na ye my he'rt was wae
>   When I turned aboot, away to gae?

> Nae living man I'll love again,
>   Since that my lovely knight is slain;
> Wi' ae lock o' his yellow hair,
>   I'll chain my he'rt for evermair.

The death longest remembered against the King is that of Johnnie Armstrong, "a gentleman . . . some time called Laird o' Gilnockie" to whom James wrote a letter "with his ain hand, sae tenderly" summoning him to his presence. Armstrongs and Elliots, a goodly company, rode together to convoy the King to a feast at Gilnockie. In the royal presence Johnnie, himself a kingly man, declared his loyalty and implored pardon for any misdeeds. The King refused:

> I grantit never a traitor's life,
>   And now I'll not begin with thee.

No offer of rich gifts (four-and-twenty milk-white steeds with as much gold as they can carry, four-and-twenty mills and all the good red wheat they can grind in a year, four-and-twenty brave lads to serve him and the rents from wide Border lands) can move the King. Still he calls Johnnie a traitor:

> "Ye lied, ye lied, now, King", he says,
>   "Altho' a King and Prince ye be!
> For I've loved naething in my life,
>   I weel dare say it, but honesty."

The King is adamant. Johnnie realises his doom:

> "I have asked grace at a graceless face,
>   But there is nane for my men and me."

> John murdered was at Carlinrigg,
>   And all his gallant companie;
> But Scotland's heart was ne'er sae wae,
>   To see sae many brave men die—

> Because they saved their country dear
>   Frae Englishmen. They were sae bauld,
> While Johnnie lived on the Border side,
>   Nane o' them durst come nigh his fauld.

These Borderers were no traitors to the King, but he lost their hearts. The trees on which Johnnie and his brave company were hanged never thereafter put forth green leaf.

The Outlaw Murray, Murray of Philiphaugh, had better luck when he met James IV.

> "The lands are Mine", the Outlaw said;
>   "I ken nae King in Christentie;
> Frae Soudron I this Forest wan,
>   When the King nor his knights were not to see."

The King coveted Ettrick:

> The fairest Forest
> That ever man saw with his e'e.

and rode against the Outlaw with a great host. The Outlaw fell on his knees:

> "Grant mercie, mercie, nobil King,
>   E'en for His Sake That died on tree."

So well did he plead his cause that the King came to terms. For Murray's fealty and that of his men, he would render him both lands and castle:

> "I'll make thee Sheriffe of Ettrick Forest,
>   Surely while upward grows the tree."

And so it was done.

> Who ever heard in ont times,
>   Sicken an Outlaw in his degree
> Sic favour get before a King,
>   As did the Outlaw Murray of the Forest free?

A wise King knew when to concede a man's just demands and secure his loyalty, when to make a pact of mutual profit. James, it is said, made one with Johnnie Faa, King of the Gipsies.

There was peril from the English over the Border, but the adventure of Kinmont Willie has a cheerful ending. Taken to Carlisle by Lord Scrope he would, no doubt, have been hanged. But the Keeper of the Border on the Scottish side was the bold Buccleuch, and he and his men, with the Elliots rode off, crossing the Eden at Stoneshaw Bank, leaving their horses there and creeping on to Carlisle Castle, where they set ladders to the walls—and up with them, Buccleuch the foremost. They blew the trumpet call: "Wha' dare meddle wi' me?" with such sound and fury that the English thought King James and all his army had come upon them; and it was only

> Twenty Scots and ten
> That put a thousand in sic a steer.

They took Willie from his dungeon and carried him off, while he called a courteous farewell to his host, promising him payment for his lodging when next he came to Scotland. And safe over Eden again, Buccleuch called a challenge:

> If ye like na my visit in merrie England,
> In fair Scotland come visit me.

Such courtesy is to be commended. Feuds need not destroy good manners among gentleman.

And the Borderers were gentlemen.

Lord Scrope accepts defeat with good sense:

> He is either himself a devil frae hell,
>   Or else his mother a witch maun be;
> I wadna hae ridden that wan water
>   For a' the gowd in Christeitie.

It is pleasant to find a eulogy on the Borderers by a Bishop: Bishop Leslie of Ross, about 1562–66.

"Shedding of blood they greatly abhor", except in revenge or self-defence, in war or a clan feud, which any gentleman can understand. No decent man kills for the sake of killing. Their supreme virtue was their good faith, shown even to a foe. They did not slay by treachery, only in clean fight. They were strong in truth, in courage, in humanity. Their recreations were music and the reciting of ballads. And that eulogy was written in a stormy period.

The magic of the ballads touches those of war as well as of the supernatural.

> It fell about the Lammas-tide,
>   When the muir men win their hay,
> The doughty Douglas bound him to ride
>   Into England to drive a prey,

and to fight against Percy and his men. It is a fatal day for him and he has foreknowledge of his doom:

> But I hae dreamed a dreary dream,
>   Beyond the Isle of Skye,
> I saw a dead man win a fight,
>   And I think that man was I. . . .
>
> . . . My wound is deep, I fain would sleep,
>   Take thou the vanguard of the three,
> And bury me by the bracken bush
>   That grows on yonder lilie lea;
>
> O bury me by the bracken bush
>   Beneath the blooming brier,
> Let never living mortal ken
>   That ere a kindly Scot lies here.

The Borders may not be unique in having so much of their history told in ballad, but they are unsurpassed in this form of record. From poetry it is a short step to history. True events are related with passion, with drama, plainly, yet with magic of phrase.

One tragedy in history inspired a ballad-like poem in a much later day, in a time of peace. Flodden remained a national grief. It was sung by Jean Elliot, in a song of the old style at once realistic and noble:

> I've heard the liltin' at our ewe-milkin',
>   Lassies a-lillin' before dawn o' day;
> But noo there's a moanin' on ilka green loanin',
>   The Floo'ers o' the Forest are a' wede away.

It recalls in every verse the pastoral life of the country.

This turmoil subsided on the Union of the Crowns; but it would be foolish and false to say that the spirit of the Borders grew cold. It has been roused in the immediate present, as will be told in a later chapter, by certain plans of development.

On the whole, however, the Borders, like the rest of Scotland, began in the late eighteenth century to cultivate the fields, to develop trade and manufacture, to share in the golden age of letters. Scott knew this world, which still remembered the old ways; he was spiritually at home in both.

III

THE BORDERS AT PRAYER

The monastic orders are known to have been ambitious of adorning their habitations with great architectural works which were frequently begun on a scale of magnificence vastly beyond their means, and which the labours of several generations were required to complete.

—The Rev. George Thomson of Melrose in
The New Statistical Account of Scotland

THE Borders have had more than a little traffic with "The Secret Commonwealth of Elves and Fairies"—to quote the title of Robert Kirk's famous treatise; they have had their fill of raids and battles; but they have long known the Christian faith, and Christian creed and worship have been expressed in some of the loveliest churches and abbeys ever built in this island.

Their chief apostle was Cuthbert, the shepherd-saint of the seventh century, whose teaching was derived from Northumberland monks who had been taught by the followers of St. Columba. Christianity had spread south from Iona to northern England, then back across the Borders into the valleys of Tweed, Ettrick and Yarrow.

Cuthbert is believed to have been born near Melrose and to have been a shepherd in his boyhood. Holiness was in him all his life and a child companion was moved to prophesy that he would be a bishop. While he watched his sheep one night he had a vision of Aidan, the Northumbrian saint's being carried up to heaven, and knew it to be the sign of the death of a holy man. This drew him into the priesthood. He went to Melrose, to the little, humble Abbey of those days, where Boisil the Prior welcomed him: "Behold the servant of the Lord." Boisil was himself to be canonised, his name, somewhat altered being commemorated in the village of St. Boswell's.

One tradition states that he was of poor parentage; this is denied by a recent biographer, the late Canon Henry Kelsey, a former Rector of the Episcopal Church in Melrose. He finds that Cuthbert was of wealthy family, that he spent his first childhood with foster-parents, and from his foster-mother Kenswith had his first Christian teaching, and adds that he came to Melrose not on foot, but riding, and attended by a servant. It makes little difference; rich or poor he knew the homely country ways; if rich he had the more to give up. But he had holy detachment always.

He was greatly loved. When he was grievously ill of the plague he was brought back to life by force of prayer on the part of the monks who knew him to be called to a great mission. When he was told of this, in the morning, Cuthbert said: "Give me my staff and shoes." He was ready to go forth on his journeys.

The shoes were to carry him, the staff to support him on many a long road through the Borders, from east to west, from Berwickshire to Solway. Stories were told of his miracles, some of them so like those of Our Lord that it may be that his vivid telling of them made people attribute to himself like actions: the turning of water into wine, the calming of the sea, and others. Long before St. Francis he showed the Franciscan love of all creatures; indeed many of the old Scottish saints had this charity and enjoyed companionship with birds and beasts and all God's creatures. Holiness called forth responsive kindness.

Cuthbert, again like those early saints of Scotland, imposed on himself severe bodily discipline. One story tells how one night he waded deep into the sea, at Coldingham, there to spend hours in penitential prayer; when he came back to the shore two otters crept up to him to dry his feet and warm them with their breath.

From Melrose where he was, for a time, Prior, he went to Lindisfarne on the Northumbrian coast, as Prior of the monastery there; some years later he withdrew to Farne Island to live in solitude and prayer; Melrose was his first home, Lindisfarne his next, and here was his hermitage, but his journeys had carried him to the westernmost corner of south Scotland, and in that corner the Stewartry and town of Kirkcudbright bear his name.

People flocked to this good shepherd of souls. Dearly as he loved his solitude of prayer he was available to them all, and he used to say that to comfort and advise the weak was an act of prayer. He had the radiance, the strength, the gentleness that we find in Ninian, in Columba and Kentigern and others of the Scottish Church, a simplicity along with his learning and authority, above all a profound charity which drew forth faith and charity from others.

One pleasant legend is of a miraculous feeding. It happened in Teviotdale near where Kelso now stands. Cuthbert had been teaching and baptising the people, and was hungry. He asked his servant to prepare a meal, but—as once in Galilee, there was no food.

"Look," Cuthbert told the boy, and the boy looked up to see an eagle high in flight; the eagle swooped down, caught a salmon in Teviot, and laid it before them. The kind saint bade half of the fish to be given to the eagle, half to be broiled for themselves.

Another story he told himself, long after it happened, to a monk who told it to the Venerable Bede, Cuthbert's first and greatest biographer. Late one night he had come riding to a deserted hut; there was shelter there, but no food for man or beast except a little straw for the latter. But as Cuthbert was saying his Office he saw his horse pull down some thatch from the roof, and with the thatch came a bundle containing enough bread and meat for his supper, with a share for the horse.

Cuthbert was a joyful saint having that essential virtue in a high degree. Bede called him "affable and pleasant in his manner"; he was full of pity for sinners, wept for his penitents, and used to celebrate Mass with tears in his eyes thinking of the Passion. Sir George Douglas calls him "the earliest and assuredly one of the worthiest of Border worthies".

He was conformable too; at the Synod of Whitby in 663 or 664, although his sympathy was with the Celtic Church in the dispute over the date of Easter, the tonsure and other matters, he accepted the rule and discipline of Rome, in order to prevent schism.

For nine years he stayed in his hermitage on Farne Island, his friend Eata being now Prior of Lindisfarne. Pilgrims flocked to him, and none went away uncomforted. Not only human pilgrims came but flocks of birds for whom he had a special tenderness. They knew it, and trusted him utterly. His favourites, the eider-ducks, St. Cuthbert's ducks, would let him stroke them in their nests.

The floodlit Melrose Abbey
Melrose Town
(overleaf) Nearing the top of the Eildon Hills

Elected Bishop of Hexham in 684 he was so reluctant to accept that it took another bishop, the King, several of his monks and several nobles to persuade him to go to York for his consecration on Easter Day, 685; and then he found he was to be bishop of his own diocese of Lindisfarne. Eata had been elected bishop there, but the two friends agreed to change sees. And so Cuthbert returned to his own country.

He took up his missionary ways again, the active pastoral work of a bishop. About this last period there are again many stories of miracles, especially of healing. He blessed a boy brought, desperately ill and weak, on a litter, and the boy arose, strong and well; he healed a woman and her son of the plague; he anointed with holy chrism a woman who suffered grievous pains in her head and side, and the pains left her.

Having spent Christmas of 686 on Lindisfarne with his sons in God, the bishop went over to his own island of Farne, to his beloved solitude; he told the brethren that he would return—when they brought his body to Lindisfarne. And so it happened. On 20th March, 687, he died in great peace, having received the Sacraments and uttered his last prayer to God. His body was brought back to Lindisfarne, but it was taken further; it lies now in Durham Cathedral.

The hermit's way was an old one, chosen by some from the first ages of Christianity. About a century before St. Cuthbert Melrose had a hermit, Drithelm, noted for his asceticism and his penances. He used to plunge up to the neck in the icy water of the river, and to any remonstrances reply that he had known cold much deadlier than that. The legend was that he had died, and known both Purgatory and Paradise, and been recalled from the dead; but of that he would not speak.

The Abbey which knew Drithelm and Cuthbert was a humble place, of much holiness, built at old Melrose on a promontory on Tweed. The Melrose and the Abbey of today began in the twelfth century, that age of the high flowering of the religious life and its expression in architecture. There was a specially rich flowering in Scotland, within a small region and a small period of time, in the reign of the devout King David I, son of Saint Margaret, Queen of Scotland and King Malcolm Canmore; he was nicknamed, by a successor "a sair sanct for the Crown" having spent so much of the royal treasury upon churches and

Jedburgh Abbey from the south

abbeys. He built Melrose Abbey in 1136, for the Cistercian monks who came over from Citeaux in France to Rievaulx in Yorkshire, then north to Melrose. It was dedicated to Our Lady.

The monastic Orders in the west are based on the Rule of St. Benedict, each with its own developments and variations. There is this one root or source; four offshoots or streams are—the Cistercians, the Tironensians, and the two Orders of Canons Regular, the Augustinians and the Premonstratensians, these latter two being more distinct than the former from the common pattern.

The Cistercians stress the rule of poverty, the withdrawal into silence. Their life includes hard, manual work, usually agricultural. They have made grass grow where none grew before, two ears of wheat where there had been but one. They dig and plough, sow and reap and build; in building their achievement has been beauty through form rather than through adornment, through richness of carved stone and painted glass. Melrose when it was first built may have had this austere loveliness; it was damaged or destroyed more than once by English marauders, and was rebuilt with enrichments to enchant the eye, though they were not in the true Cistercian tradition. Melrose is exuberant; enough has survived of the carvings to show its florescence: flowers and foliage, heads and figures, human or animal: a man telling his beads, a pig playing the bagpipes, a fat mason, no doubt portrait or caricature of one of the workmen; the pig must have been done for the fun of it.

The chief mason was one John Morow who has left an inscription on a wall in the south transept, one which is both record and prayer:

> John Morow sum tyne called was I,
> And born in Parysse certainly,
> And had in keepyng all masoun work
> Of Santandrys ye hye kirk,
> Of Glasgow, Melrose and Pasley,
> Of Nyddysdale and of Galway;
> I pray to God and Mary baith,
> And sweet Saint John keep this haly kirk frae skaith.

His prayer was not granted; both kirk and abbey took great skaith or harm, even before the onslaught of the Reformers.

On a tombstone in the churchyard is carved this pungent version of *Sic Transit Gloria Mundi*:

> The earth goeth upon the earth glistering like gold,
> The earth goeth to the earth sooner than it wold;
> The earth buildeth on the earth castles and towers,
> The earth sayeth to the earth: All shall be ours.

And so much of proud and lovely Melrose came crumbling down to the earth.

The English began it in the Border wars, reaching their climax of destruction in the sixteenth century with Surrey and his army. The Reformers continued the work of destruction with holy glee: "The wark o' God gangs bonnily on" as was said by a later devastator. Doubtless there had been corruption, a falling away, with ample excuse for mockery. Scott gives an example:

> The monks of Melrose made gude kale
> On Fridays, when they fasted,
> They wanted neither beef nor ale
> As long as their neighbours' lasted.

The fat monk was a figure of satire long before fat Luther made his protest and quitted his monastery.

But against some corruption and negligence must be set infinite good, done by work and prayer, by teaching and beneficence, by cultivation of the land, by fostering trade, including the master trade of the Borders, that of woollens. In 1225, the Abbot of Melrose sent Border wool to Flanders to be woven by the expert weavers there. In the next century, between 1370 and 1394 the Abbots were regular wool-dealers and exporters, being granted exemption from duty. The rest of that story belongs to the history of the wool-trade, but it was the monks who began it. They were good shepherds of their four-footed flock as well as of the human souls under their charge. After all, St. Cuthbert had herded his sheep before he came to the Abbey. And the monks kept order. George Scott Moncrieff justly claims that "the decline of the abbeys saw the rise of the Border reivers"—though there would always have been some cattle-lifting, raiding and clan rivalry.

The depredations begun by the English, continued by the Reformers were cannily taken over by the neighbours with little malice or theological hatred, but with strict regard to themselves and disregard of the rule of *meum* and *tuum*. Stones and carvings, whatever was portable were lifted and taken home by douce townsfolk to adorn a lintel or a chimney-piece.

Kelso was Tironsensian, of a religious family close akin to the Cistercians, founded by a Cistercian monk, Bernard of Poitiers, who withdrew to a life of solitude and prayer in the Forest of Tiron near Chartres. His followers and spiritual descendants continued the Cistercian rule and discipline, their mingling of manual work with the Opus Dei of prayer and liturgic worship. Their work was that of the craftsman rather than of the fieldworker, and they attracted craftsmen and artisans of all kinds. For them King David built this abbey in a style mainly Romanesque, strong, almost austere. Stewart Cruden in his account of *The Scottish Abbeys* says it is "characterised by a powerful simplicity", comparing it with Ely. In this simplicity it would appear to be more Cistercian than Melrose of the exuberant, late-mediaeval fantasies.

The other two Orders were less strictly cloistered: the Augustinians or Black Canons (from their habit) who settled at Jedburgh, and the Premonstratensians or White Canons (again from their habit) of Dryburgh, both Abbeys built and endowed by the Sair Sanct. In their way of life the Benedictine Rule was adapted to the increasing need for active evangelisation. They were preaching monks, like those of St. Cuthbert's day, going out from their monasteries, from field and library and scriptorium into the towns, to preach the Gospel. In this way they were forerunners of the Preaching Friars of St. Francis and St. Dominic, as they were successors of the old missionary monks.

Both Jedburgh and Dryburgh are most happily placed, and the beauty of their setting could not be destroyed. Jedburgh was built above the river, descending in terraces, and much of its loveliness remains. Dryburgh is set among lawns and trees, with a good deal of building left; enough to show the lay-out of cloisters and chapter-house, sacristy, parlour, library; a great cupboard with grooves for shelves, the stair leading from chapter-house to dortoir or dormitory, the infirmary, the warming house. Central heating in some form was known to the monks, and there was running water in a cistern.

In Jedburgh as in Melrose there is record of an earlier church, founded from Lindisfarne. The later priory, which became an abbey, was built in 1118, and the first monks or Canons came over from Beauvais. Jedburgh too was sorely battered by the English, though stoutly defended by Jeddart men with their Jeddart staves, effective weapons, being poles eight feet long, tipped with a hook or an axe. The abbey was finally destroyed by Surrey and his men, not without suffering on their part.

"The boldest men and the hottest that ever I saw in any nation", he said of these adversaries, adding that if the strength of Teviotdale were broken, only a small force would be needed to keep the Borders under subjection to England.

Dryburgh owes its foundation to a noble knight, Hugh de Morville, who gave it to the Premonstratensians from Northumberland in 1152. Through his father's kindred Scott inherited his right and place of burial here.

Stewart Cruden in his excellent book on the abbeys has pointed out that the architecture of these four is European, not Scottish; only in the fifteenth century is a national form of architecture found in Scottish churches. Monastic life was at once enclosed, secluded, withdrawn, and international, without boundaries. It was also extremely well planned.

"The more one studies the monastic plan" (again to quote Stewart Cruden) "the more does one marvel at its sheer efficiency."

It was truly a design for living a life built on solid foundations of common sense as well as devotion. The monks made their own way of life, their own inner world within that of ordinary people; they were in touch with that, they were not remote. It was a full life of work and worship, prayer, study, contemplation, agriculture, craftsmanship, writing, eating, sleeping, hospitality to guests, care of the sick and poor, teaching, healing. They were active as well as contemplative. It is not realistic, it is mere whimsy to picture them utterly withdrawn from the bustle of life into some lovely rural fastness. If they withdrew it was not to escape from life, but to live more fully one particular kind of life.

Scott noted that the Borderers retained allegiance to the Old Religion longer than other parts of Scotland, such as the southwest (though not continually, to the present day, like some parts of the Highlands). He added that this was due less to piety than to their "total indifference upon the subject". There was little zeal for the new doctrines. Borderers had other matters of concern, regarding themselves, their families, their sheep and other possessions, their enemies in other clans or over the Border. They had little time for theology. Scott, a tolerant man himself, writes with pungent cynicism about sectarian passion. When the "flame of Reformation" had reached "the violence of a volcanic eruption" the Lords of the Congregation allied themselves against Mary of Guise, the Queen Regent, with the English. There was a good deal of English gold coming north. "The Borderers cared little about speculative points of religion; but they showed much interest in the treasures which passed through their country for payment of the English forces. Much alarm was excited lest the Marchers should intercept those weighty Protestant arguments". Scott's own Border blood may explain his own tepid response to zealots.

He moved away from the strict Presbyterianism of his boyhood and home to the Episcopal Church he loved for its beauty of liturgy, its mellower ways, its great tradition, finding it closer than any other to the purity of the primitive Church of the first centuries. In Scotland Episcopacy had suffered much persecution, especially since the Forty-five, for allegiance to the Stuarts; it had come to be what Peter Pleydell in *Guy Mannering* called "the shadow of a shade". In Scott's day this "ancient and suffering Church" had gained her freedom, increasing tolerance, and was beginning to approach some prosperity. After his day there was a marked renewal, as there was in the Roman Communion also. Episcopal churches were built in the Border towns: St. John the Evangelist, Jedburgh was the first, consecrated in 1844. Keble was present at the consecration and the church grew in the old Scottish Episcopal tradition renewed by the Oxford Movement. Holy Trinity, Melrose, came next in 1849, then St. Peter's, Galashiels in 1854, St. Cuthbert's, Hawick in 1858, St. John's, Selkirk and St. Andrew's, Kelso were both consecrated in 1869, but the Episcopalian congregation in Kelso has a long history, though the documentary records have been lost, going back to 1690.

The Border gentry were many of them Episcopalian, and the two great patrons of the Church were the Duke of Buccleuch and the Marquis of Lothian. After the early death of Lord Lothian his widow continued the devout work, and it was through her generosity that the church in Jedburgh was built. The Duke of Buccleuch built a chapel in Dalkeith, and was patron of the

Church in Hawick. The Duchess and Lady Lothian, devoted friends and devout Anglicans became troubled by doubts of the Catholicism of their Church, and in the early 1850s both were received into the Roman Communion. There was a flood of conversions about this time; among other converts were the Hope-Scotts of Abbotsford. They and Lady Lothian were again builders of churches in the Border towns. The Old Religion came again to the Borders. It was not, as in some parts of Scotland, an influx from another country, nor indeed was Episcopacy. In Glasgow, for example, Catholicism grew immensely by the arrival of Irish work-people. But the Border Catholics were as Scottish as their Presbyterian neighbours, and the Episcopalians were, most of them, not English who had come north, but Scots who held by or had returned to Episcopacy.

The great majority of people were Presbyterian, of the Established Church or one of the dissident sects. Our next chapter will be told largely from the reports of the parish ministers.

IV

SEEN BY THE CLERGY

SCOTT died in 1832, and in the next few years *The New Statistical Account of Scotland* was prepared and published, most of the records, like those in the earlier Account of 1795, written by the parish ministers, those of the counties of Roxburgh, Selkirk and Peebles chiefly compiled in the 1830s—when Scott was a living memory, his country unchanged from what he had known though with changes in sight. They make excellent social history, and most of them make good reading as well, often entertaining, indicative of the character of the writers who, though factual and nearly always objective, are also human. An occasional comment reveals the individual.

The minister of Smailholm recalls Scott's childhood at Sandy-knowe in his parish, refers to his description of the old Tower in "The Eve of St. John", and adds that the village "though small, is not isolated; the Tweedside coach between Kelso and Edinburgh passes through every lawful day, at 9 a.m. going north, at 2 p.m. going south; every Monday, the Earlston carrier collects eggs and butter for the Edinburgh market, which is of great advantage to the neighbourhood."

These carriers with their carts were important persons in the rural economy, long after this date, taking produce to the market towns and to the cities, bringing back parcels for their country customers.

The minister adds: "There are an inn and an alehouse in the village. Their effect on the morals of the people is decidedly un-favourable"—which covers a good deal. This comment, in one form or other, occurs in many of the reports. Ale and whisky were cheap, and the Scot has a large capacity.

Kelso is described in detail, with an eloquence in which we may hear an echo of Scott's remembrances. The scenery "belongs,

Mary Queen of Scots' house in Jedburgh

indeed, to the class of the beautiful rather than the romantic. . . .
It may be questioned if Scotland contains a spot superior to it in
its own style of beauty."

The term "romantic" suggested at that time a rugged and
sombre grandeur. Scott had called Kelso "the most beautiful if
not the most romantic village in Scotland". Now, considerably
more than a village:

"It can boast a square of no inconsiderable size and some architectural pretensions. And its houses throughout being built of a
light-coloured stone and roofed with blue slate, impart to the
place an elegant and city-like air".

There is about Kelso something of the aspect of a French provincial town. Scotland's towns and villages are often far inferior
to the scenery of their background; the old and picturesque
among them can too easily be counted. When elegance does
appear, it calls for emphasis. Perhaps the river is the secret of
Kelso's charm—can a town be really beautiful without one?
Certainly one that has a stream or river running through it cannot be dull or commonplace. Kelso has the confluence of Teviot
with Tweed. Leyden, the poetic scholar of the Borders, friend of
Scott, has celebrated this meeting of the waters:

> Teviot, farewell! For now thy silver tide
> Commixed with Tweed's pellucid stream shall glide.
> But all thy green and pastoral beauties fail
> To match the softness of thy parting vale.
> Bosomed in woods where mighty rivers run,
> Kelso's fair vale expands before the sun . . .
> . . . Blue o'er the river Kelso's shadow lies,
> And copse-clad isles amid the waters rise. . . .
>
> Yet, sure, these pastoral beauties ne'er can vie
> With those that fondly rise to Memory's eye,
> When absent long, my soul delights to dwell
> On scenes, in early youth she loved so well.
> 'Tis fabling Fancy, with her radiant hues,
> That gilds the modest scenes which Memory views.

To return to sober clerical prose, the minister refers with pride
to Kelso's wealth of history and tradition; then speaking in his
best pulpit manner:

"The visitor whose associations take the direction of devotion

West doorway of Abbey Kirk, Dryburgh Abbey

rather than of poetry, will find here ample food for the enviable habit of mind which, by connecting the idea of Deity with all the objects and aspects of Nature, causes the landscape to become tributary not only to the imagination but to piety."

It may be noted that the good ministers of these Border parishes value the heritage of the old faith.

This particular cleric does not lack geniality. He corrects Scott's interpretation of the phrase "a Kelso convoy". Scott had said it meant seeing a guest to the front door. The minister declares that it meant escorting him to his own front door then being escorted back again; a convivial process.

There was scope for conviviality. Kelso had sixty-three inns or ale-houses, one for every eighteen males of the population. Most of the grocers, too, were licensed.

"The baleful practice of selling drams across their counters" with the tea and sugar was "one of the most fertile occasions of drunkenness". (Chesterton said the same thing about two hundred years later and said it in rhyme.) It was easy to obtain a license, easy to set up a small pub:

"Out of the many reputable and exemplary persons who take to tavern keeping as a refuge from reduced circumstances, there is scarcely one who does not, in the course of a few years, sink down into an incurable and habitual sot". Harsh words, but harsher facts!

This is the black spot on a picture otherwise pleasant and comely. The minister thinks well of his people, on the whole, well-living folk, advancing in comfort and prosperity:

"In respect of cleanliness, clothing and general style and manner of living, the inhabitants—the class of gipsies and the more improvident of the paupers excepted—are justly considered to surpass most rural populations. A taste for neatness of dress, well-furnished houses, and other domestic comforts is very general; nay is, in some instances, carried to excess."

They may not have had our system of hire purchase but they liked their comforts and what they did not call their status symbols, and sometimes ran into debt for them.

"The dress of the females is in all cases neat; that of female servants (in particular) showy to an extent which might be advantageously abated."

Set them up!—to use a homely Scoticism—copying their

betters, putting most of their wages on their backs and their heads! This may well have been mentioned in the pulpit, and now was the chance to put it into print.

Apart from such vanity, and the deplorable tendency to drunkenness, there was no great evil to report:

"The moral character of a population of 5000 souls [this included the whole parish, not only the town of Kelso] is, like their habits, necessarily various. But as a whole, the people are sober and industrious, amiable in the relations of life, and attentive to their religious duties."

With an agreeable touch of local patriotism the minister adds:

"They are more polished in manners, and respectful to all above them than persons of the same station in manufacturing towns, though perhaps somewhat inferior in acuteness of mind and extent of general information."

It was a virtue to know one's station in life and to order oneself lowly and reverently towards one's betters. And yet there was no subservience. The Scot, rich or poor, of high or humble rank, remains a person; and in the country there was less resentment of class distinction and privilege, less cultivation of the chip on the shoulder.

There were of course lapses from virtue, resulting in illegitimate births. More common, less reprehensible though far from laudable were the irregular marriages, performed at Coldstreambridge, for a fee, by a bankrupt tradesman. These were legal by Scots law which is convenient for those desiring to be married in haste, but they were not approved. Couples thus married were admonished by the Kirk Session before being restored to full church privileges.

Living was frugal among the poorer folk who rarely ate meat, but more often pork; the commonest fish was herring; the staple fare consisted of oatmeal, milk and potatoes. Bread was baked of wheaten flour, sometimes with a mixture of pease and barley meal. In the town there might be a greater variety for those who could afford it, but the very poor were worse off without a bit of a garden for growing kale.

The town of Kelso had some 4,200 inhabitants of whom twenty-five were professional men: six ministers, eight doctors, eleven lawyers. There were some manufactures: linen weaving, leather work, the making of a coarse woollen cloth, but most of the townspeople were tradesmen or shopkeepers. In the country the farms were many of them prosperous, with good buildings, well-kept dykes and hedges, and with modern implements. Farm labourers were paid from 1s. 6d. to 1s. 8d. a day, ploughmen £3 10s. a year, but this, the minister estimated, was brought up to about £27 by their allowance of free oats, barley, pease and potatoes, a free house, pasture and winter keep for a cow, and free coal. In return the ploughman must provide, besides his own service, that of an extra worker in the harvest. This was usually his wife, with another female labourer, called bondagers, for whom he was paid 8d. or 10d. a day. The other bondager was often one of his own children.

There was much pasture land. On the whole Kelso was comfortable and respectable, with plenty of work to offer. There was some poverty, there was some immorality, but illegitimacy was decreasing; "whilst the increase of benefit clubs and of savings banks deposits indicates that along with the abandonment of a worse, there is a return on the part of the common people to a better course of feeling and conduct";—a very Scottish conjunction of virtue and thrift.

The well-to-do did not forget their duty to the poor: "Among the most marked characteristic of all classes, especially the higher, may be specified beneficence to the poor, a large spirit of hospitality, and a strong feeling of local attachment." This last is still true of the Border towns. The Borderer is a loyal citizen of Great Britain, a loyal Scot, but within that larger fealty lies an intense local pride, in the Borders, in his own town or valley, in local history and achievements. He is still proudly aware of his heritage.

"It is difficult to persuade a native that there is any town prettier than Kelso."

The minister would hardly admit it himself: Kelso people "form a little community which, in point of general intelligence and polish of manners, may claim a place beside that of the most favoured rural districts in the island".

There was poverty, but there were few beggars. Poor relief was administered by the Kirk Session. Some of the very poor "were allowed to go round the town of a Saturday, for a small gratuity which particular families are in the habit of bestowing on them". In such households there would be the announcement: "Here's Auld Wullie" or "Auld Maggie" and the poor creature would be given a penny, perhaps a warm cast-off garment, in the kindlier houses brought to the kitchen fire and given a bowl of broth or a cup of tea. Edie Ochiltree and his kind were passing; Scott would have regretted their departure. Sturdy beggars or gaberlunzies had once done very well for themselves; there was record of one who could collect as much as fourteen shillings in one day.

The Society for the Suppression of Mendicity was putting a stop to this, for subscribers were pledged "not to give charity to any vagrants who might apply" but to make all their donations to the Society who had an office in the town; here, mendicants might come for help and be given alms or a free lodging for the night on condition of leaving the town next day.

Kelso had a dispensary for the sick poor, and a hospital for fever patients with one room set aside for operations. Social welfare was already a concern for the benevolent.

It was a kirk-going town, most of the people adhering to the Church of Scotland, some to the various Presbyterian sects, a few to Episcopacy. And these were, in town and country, no fewer than ten schools, including a girls' school, two boarding-schools for young ladies (a nice distinction) and one for young gentlemen. In the Grammar School, where Scott had attended for a season, Latin, Greek and French were taught as were as the elementary subjects. At their boarding-schools the young ladies might acquire "the ornamental branches of education" such as music and drawing.

This is an impressive list, but attendance at school, not yet compulsory, was declining; this was due, in the case of some genteel families, to a preference for having their children taught at home by tutor or governess or visiting masters; at the other end of the scale, to poverty and the need to send children out to work; but most of all it was due to indifference "strengthened by the loss of self-respect which a habit of asking and taking indiscriminate charity engenders".

Teachers were poorly paid; in some schools partly by endowment, partly by pupils' fees which might range from a penny a week to a guinea a quarter. In spite of this deplorable indifference, however, Kelso was a place of considerable culture, with a reading public. The Kelso Library had flourished since 1750; we hear about it in the Journal of the Reverend George Ridpath who was minister of the neighbouring parish of Stitchell at that time: he used to ride into Kelso, spend many happy hours in the library and carry home a load of books. Now, in the 1830s there were about 5,000 volumes for the seventy subscribers. The New Library and the Modern Library had, respectively about 2,000 and 1,500 books. Some of the churches ran a Sunday School library, and for country dwellers there was a travelling book-van, part of the East Lothian Itinerating Library, "lately introduced for the benefit of the working classes".

For the gentry there was, besides the Kelso Library, a book-club kept up by twenty-four members, each paying a guinea subscription; the books, after being circulated, were sold, and the money used to buy new publications. This club "has very materially contributed, both by the kind of works it has circulated and by the intercourse it has kept up among the members, to maintain a taste for literature in the town and neighbourhood".

This gives a pleasant picture of meetings in the club room or a bookshop to exchange books; of genial evenings in the members' houses in turn, with talk about books, local gossip, political discussion, followed by a cup of tea and slice of home-baked cake or piece of shortbread, and possibly something a trifle stronger and more mellowing to the organ.

This particular *Account* was written in 1838 when Scott had been dead for six years but was still a loved and recently known personality. Lockhart's *Life* had appeared and must have been discussed at length and in detail.

There were, besides, two reading-rooms for the perusal of newspapers and periodicals; one "of considerable standing, belonging to a select society of gentlemen", the other open to all who could pay the subscription.

"It is to the honour of the latter that, by an express regulation, it is shut on the Lord's Day". Did the Gentlemen's Reading-room stay open on the Sabbath, the gentry sitting more easily to Sabbatical discipline, and did members look in after church (none would be so lost to grace as to appear before service) to hear the latest news from town and exchange gossip? In these rooms the newspapers from Edinburgh and London could be seen as well as the excellent local *Kelso Mail* and *Kelso Journal*.

The town had two deliveries of letters a day—one from the southern, one from the northern mailbag; we are no better off today. Kelso had no mail-coach of its own, but letter carts carried the mail-bags to and from the mail-town, Hawick. Stage coaches ran between Kelso and the other Border towns, and Edinburgh, Newcastle and London. Carriers conveyed heavy goods. There were good bridges over Tweed and Teviot; but there was no sign yet of the long-promised much-needed railway. On this the minister was caustic:

"The Kelso and Berwick railroad from which such extensive benefits were long anticipated to Tweedside and Teviotdale, has existed for the past twenty years in an Act of Parliament, and in the pages of The Travellers' Guide. Why it does not yet exist in any more tangible and useful shape, and is not likely to do so, is best known to the shareholders who, judged from their past proceedings, appear to have been incorporated for the purpose of defeating, not of carrying into effect, the provisions of an Act of Parliament."

Kelso, once called the Melton of Scotland, was still addicted to field sports, to hunting, fishing and racing. The salmon-fishing was famous, there was a local Hunt, and "once a year, the whip-men of the Border turn out, horse and rider gaily tricked out with ribbons and silken sashes, to ride a race which is the great delight of the rustics and schoolboys."

For the boys, the favourite game was football. At Candlemas a boy was chosen to be head of the school or king of the feast like the king on Twelfth Night. It was often the one who had made "the most liberal Candlemas offering" to the Grammar School. To him the headmaster or rector presented a football "which becomes a source of amusement to the whole pupils for several weeks afterwards".

The minister approved of the boys' fun; indeed he deplored, good man, the lack of games and sport among the poorer people. For this "the intoxication of political excitement" was partly to blame, but still more blameworthy were the long hours of work.

"Is it not to the disgrace of this great and wealthy nation that the bulk of the working classes should require to spend so many hours of the day in toil, as to have no leisure either for the culture of their minds, or for the improvement of that physical vigour which is almost essential to a cheerful and contented frame of mind".

A wise and good shepherd of his flock!

Jedburgh, also known from its river as Jedwood and Jedworth, also had a good report from its minister. A healthy place, many of its inhabitants lived to be eighty, some to ninety, one had lived to a hundred. The most distinguished nonagenarian had been a former minister of the parish, Dr. Somerville, who died in 1830; one of the best of Border worthies, scholar, historian, much-loved pastor.

He was also a delightful autobiographer, and his *Life and Times* has vivid portraits of himself, his people, his world. Distinguished himself he gains further distinction as uncle and father-in-law of that learned and charming lady, Mary Somerville, mathematician and astronomer, from whom Oxford named Somerville College. More of him later.

The old Forest had, by this *Account*, been "rapaciously cut down" in the past century, but it was still a well-wooded district, with a few trees from the ancient woods, including the two oaks, The Capon Tree and The King of the Wood about a mile from the town. The great Jedburgh game was, and still is, the Handball, played vigorously and ritually on Fastern E'en or Shrove Tuesday.

The town was pleasantly situated, wide and clean, with some good shops "in which all the necessities and most of the luxuries of life can be purchased". Manufactures included blankets, flannels, plaids, shawls and hosiery. The working day in the mills and factories was from ten to twelve hours, any longer being found "unprofitable to the employer and injurious to the labourer".

Coaches ran every day to Edinburgh and to Newcastle, twice a week to Kelso and Hawick. There was a good grammar school in the town with a number of parish schools in the country-side. As in most of the Border towns, there were lending libraries, with "itinerating libraries" or book-vans about the neighbourhood, and, as in Kelso, there was a book club for the gentry.

The wages were equal to those in other parts of the country, "but are by no means a fair remuneration". The industrial age, with its problems and harshness, was beginning. The minister, like many of his fellow-clergy, was unlikely to be radical in politics, probably a sound Tory, but he and others were sympathetically aware of conditions. Jedburgh had an iron and brass foundry and a manufactory of printing presses; both they and the mills were healthy enough, "no instance having occurred of any individual being obliged to withdraw on account of ill health". The workers had, moreover, the benefit of clean country air; their leisure, however scant, could be passed in the fields and woods, by the river; they could grow and eat fruit and vegetables, they were not packed into slum tenements as in the great cities. "The effect on morals is not so favourable. Children entering at the age of nine, only partially instructed in reading, have little opportunity of acquiring religious knowledge."

The poor were helped by the parish church, from alms, parish funds and legacies, extra help being given in illness or other distress of circumstance; there was a dispensary in the town, founded by the Lothian family, and the late Marquis had built a hospital "with baths and other accommodations" where patients came from the surrounding parishes, and people could be given medicine and treatment. Besides the official parish poor relief there were "two widows' schemes, and three friendly societies", but "the general impression regarding them seems to be that they are productive of little advantage". And what lies behind that statement and what followed its appearance in print we should like to know.

The Border ministers though sound Protestants and Presbyterians without a whiff of Popery were not bigots; they valued the abbeys. Jedburgh is described in detail and with pride: "The chief object of architectural interest in this abbey is the Norman door. . . . This, for the elegance of its workmanship and the symmetry of its proportions, is unrivalled in Scotland. Its sculptured mouldings springing from slender shafts, with capitals richly wreathed, exhibit the representations of flowers, men and various animals, executed with surprising minuteness and delicacy". He quotes an architect's report that Jedburgh is "the most perfect and beautiful example of the Saxon and early Gothic in Scotland" and he notes its harmony with its setting in "the romantic valley" of Jed Water.

He is proud of the town's antiquities and memorials; of the discovery of Roman and Saxon coins, of a medal commemorating the marriage of Mary Queen of Scots with Francis the Dauphin, of a camp-kettle, of arrowheads and urns. Queen Mary's house was well preserved. Near the town were traces of Roman camps, and there were many towers and peels.

All around was the lovely pastoral and orchard country. Jedburgh was still famous for its pear-trees, as in the days of the "intelligent ecclesiastics who inhabited the monastery" and as Doroth Wordsworth discovered. Some of the trees might be three hundred years old. Apples grew well in the rich black soil, and the sheltered orchards.

The town had its proud history, and more recently its celebrities. The Grammer School had educated some famous men—Samuel Rutherford, among them, and James Thomson the poet. As for the average folk, they were "in general, intelligent, sober, orderly and industrious". Cheap spirits had led to more drinking with bad results but less evil than might have been expected. What was much to be deplored was the decline, almost the disappearance of the small farms in the countryside. Where once there had been five or six small holdings, each supporting a family, there was now one large farm. This, although a benefit to agriculture, as were the Farmers' Club and the Roxburghshire Horticultural Society, had some ill effects, depriving the community "of some of its most valuable members, by reducing them to the necessity of emigration. It has lowered the character of the peasantry, and promoted the increase of pauperism".

The people spoke the old Border Scots with some local variations, but it was giving way to English; to a corrupt form, too, which "is scarcely to be regarded as an improvement". Such a lament is common; but Scots is still spoken on the Borders, being not yet wholly forgotten.

In Melrose the minister, the Reverend George Thomson, writes almost lyrically of its setting beneath the Eildons:

"In winter, when the sun rises immediately behind them, one of the most splendid of mountain phenomena may be seen in perfection—the black, opaque mass of the hills cutting across the bright, gleaming sky." He notes the contrast of this ruggedness with the rich pastoral scenery of the valley; he loved the view from the Eildons: to the north lie Tweed, Melrose with its clustering houses and its Abbey, its woods, and beyond them "the view . . . prolonged in pastoral wildness to the distant heights of the Lammermoor, Soltra and Yarrow braes". Southward lie Teviotdale with "the long, blue line of the Cheviots" on the horizon, and at the end of the ridge, Flodden Hill of bitter memory.

Melrose was healthy and mild in climate; the common illnesses were rheumatism and tuberculosis; once there had been outbreaks of ague, but these had ceased with the draining of the marshes.

The Abbey has been "seldom surpassed or even equalled in the fineness of the sculpture, the exquisite finishing of its most minute embellishments, and the majestic beauty so suitable to a sacred edifice". The minister notes the abundance of relics and memorrials in the town and countryside: a door lintel carved with the sacred monogram; monastic names such as Cloister Close, Prior's Wood, Abbotsford; wells and springs bearing the names of saints: St. Mary's, St. Helen's, St. William's, St. Dunstan's. The people however were almost too Protestant to please him. At the passing of the Catholic Relief Act their disapproval was so strong that they could "neither get a night's rest nor a day's ease".

There were relics of a faith older than Catholicism: a tumulus on a hillside was pointed out as the site of a pagan altar; in another place an altar stone had been found inscribed by one Curius Domitianus of the Twentieth Legion to the woodland god Sylvanus: *Pro salute sua et suorum*—for his welfare and that of his family.

Now, however, Melrose was Christian in a douce way:

"It may be truly said that they are an intellectual, moral and religious people", most of them adhering to the Established Church, with a few Episcopalians, a few Seceders. Since the Reformation there had been eleven parish ministers. The second had been a nephew of John Knox, with, apparently, a good deal of the avuncular character. His successor went so far in reaction towards Catholicism or an appearance of Catholicism that he was deposed, but not before he had brought into use his own private litany:

"From the knock-down race of Knoxes, Good Lord deliver us."

Melrosians were "a stout, muscular, well-formed race, hardy and patient of fatigue", most of them sound in mind as in body; there were two insane persons among them, apparently unconfined, probably harmless; and two "fatuous"—defined by Lord Erskine in his *Institutes of the Law of Scotland* as "idiots who are entirely deprived of reason, and have a uniform stupidity and inattention in their manner, and childishness in their speech". On the whole it was a comfortable place:

"The dress of the common people . . . is always becoming and in good repair, and on particular occasions, when they appear in their 'Sunday best' it differs very little from that of the upper classes."

Naturally frugal, industrious and temperate they were further improved by education which has "in this part of the country enabled the people to find in reading a cheap and innocent amusement at their own fireside, increasing the comforts of home". Besides the town school there was a scattering of little schools about the country, and sometimes a group of families would combine to pay a teacher who would be "comfortably lodged with the principle person in the cottage group, to whom he is an agreeable companion, and to whose children he privately gives additional attention". What the children thought of this is not recorded. Such a teacher might be "a pious, old, intelligent person in decayed circumstances" or "a young aspirant after a higher school" earning his keep while he studied. In Melrose, the schoolmaster who taught Latin, Greek and French had £30 a year with a house. Melrose had a subscription library, and there were "some small religious libraries" in the villages, while hardly a cottage was without a few books, such as lay in the window-seat of the parlour at Sandyknowe.

Melrose had three fairs: in May, in August at Lammas which was a sheep fair almost rivalling that at St. Boswell's, and at Martinmass. Virtue and respectability reigned, in spite of no fewer than thirty inns and ale-houses" of which the effects on the morals of the people are most pernicious". The respectable far out-numbered the rogues. It was an honest place. Smuggling was unknown, and as for the more likely rural offence of poaching, there was a certain tolerance on the part of the landowners and magistrates:

"The parties seem to be upon honour with each other—the one not poaching beyond a certain extent, the other not pushing the enforcement of the law so far as prosecution."

The immediate neighbourhood was pastoral; the wool-manufacture lay over the river, at Galashiels, the old linen-weaving industry was defunct, the bleaching-ground now a grazing-field.

And so, over the river by the new bridge, we come into Selkirkshire, to Galashiels rapidly growing into a modern town with mills and factories and new houses.

The wool was made into blankets, plaids and flannels; the importing of fine, foreign wool was producing fine and soft material. Some of that wool could be spun out to almost incredible length; a pound of wool yielding almost thirty-seven miles of thread. Blanket-shawls, ranging in price from three to thirty shillings were much worn, and were "of so many colours and so full of comfort as to make a bad day desirable". The brilliance of *haute couture* for which modern Galashiels provides material had not yet lit the mills, but already "a gleam of fashion, like a May sun, has given a new stir to the working bees of this town".

Children were employed in the mills, often for ten or eleven hours a day, and paid sixpence in wages. Poor parents sent some of their family to school, others to the mills, turn about; there were always some earning a sixpence, while none was wholly deprived of education. Of this habit the minister approved. These children were being well prepared for a useful adult life. Of their need for sleep and play nothing is said: "There can be no training for the volatile minds of youth equal to that which is maintained at the factories". This cleric is less amiable than his colleagues in Jedburgh and Kelso.

The town had a good school, good lending libraries, and some contact with the outer world through the Edinburgh–Carlisle mail-coach which passed through; but a railroad was much needed.

South of Galashiels the county town of Selkirk was rich in history, and on this the minister likes to expatiate. Mungo Park had been born here, and of course Scott, the Sheriff had made it famous and familiar beyond the Borders.

"But the event dwelt on with the greatest complacency by the people of Selkirk is the battle of Flodden-field."

"Complacency" seems hardly the word for remembrance of so great a tragedy; but pride there truly was in the popular memory and celebration of that day when of the hundred who rode out, only four or five returned, one bearing a captured flag, still cherished by the Incorporation of Weavers to which he belonged. Since then there had been other battles, notably that of Philiphaugh only a mile away, where Montrose had been defeated by Leslie's Covenanters. At Newark on Yarrow there was The Slain Man's Lee where, it was said, the victors had put to death many of their prisoners. For a minister of the kirk to record a bloody deed done by those commonly held to be saints, shows admirable objectivity.

"Since that period Selkirk has been undistinguished by any occurrences claiming to be remembered in a compilation like the present." So the minister turns to the present.

"The habits of the people are cleanly, their houses comfortable and kept in good order. . . . Strangers invariably remark the neat and decent appearance of the lower orders on Sundays."

The emphasis on cleanliness in more than one report can be understood when one remembers the lack of running water and sanitation in houses far above the line of dire poverty. Water had usually to be fetched from the well. The standard of living was fairly high; people had wholesome food; there were "few families that have not butcher-meat every day for dinner"—a sign of adequate means. They were "much addicted to the smoking of tobacco" and (*post hoc, propter hoc?*) they were "well-informed, disposed to religion, sober and respectful".

The Grammar School has a great reputation. Latin and Greek, French and Italian were taught as well as the rudiments of education, with drawing and astronomy for good measure. Adult education was continued through reading, the local libraries being well stocked. The parish and grammar schools of Scotland where the poorest boy could learn enough to take him, with a bursary, to college, have been deservedly praised. The story of those libraries has yet to be written, their virtue to be duly celebrated. Their readers included not only the minister, the lawyer and other professional men and their wives, but the cottagers and labourers who many of them had a love of learning.

Selkirk had fifteen inns, but was fairly sober; the inns "have not, of late been much encouraged". Neither, on the other hand, was the Temperance Society. The Souters of Selkirk did not, apparently, go to either extreme of sobriety or inebriety.

Yet there was still a touch of the old lawlessness about them; the reivers' blood was in their veins. There was a good deal of poaching which was "too often the forerunner of offences of a deeper dye". Gangsters were not unknown. It is not told how they were punished. The town gaol was not strictly guarded. Of the seven prisoners confined during the past year, two had escaped, while others had the habit "of coming out in the evening, and returning again before the jailor's visit in the morning".

That might be taken as sign of a civil and co-operative spirit on the part of the prisoners. What happened during the night is not suggested. They may have joined a poaching gang with the feeling of being in for a penny, in for a pound, or they may have gone doucely home to their families.

Yarrow, as its minister proudly recalls, was very much in Scott's own country; his ancestress had been known, for her beauty, as the Flower of Yarrow, his maternal grandfather, Dr. John Rutherford, son of a minister of the parish, had been called The Yarrow Doctor with much local pride in his skill. He had gone to Edinburgh in 1727 as Professor of the Practice of Physic. Dr. Rutherford was the pioneer of clinical instruction to his students.

From another kinsman, Colonel Russell, Scott had rented Ashestiel on the edge of the parish of Yarrow: "A small hillock, covered with trees, beneath whose shade much of his poetry was penned, is still called 'The Shirra's Knowe'." His friend and fellow-poet and collector of ballads, James Hogg, the Ettrick Shepherd, was a son of Yarrow.

There had been much change in husbandry and economy in the past thirty or forty years. The black-faced sheep had given place to the Cheviot, there was no longer any ewe-milking as in the song. Agriculture was much improved, with drainage of the land, and with rotation of crops. Better cottages were being built, roads were improved, and as a result there was more transport, bringing a variety of goods: "What used to be the luxuries have become the necessaries of life". It was good that the people should be better fed, better clothed, better housed, but the change in the old ways was not altogether welcome. Much of the old lore and tradition was being forgotten and lost. "The legends of superstition are in great measure forgotten, and its rites forsaken". As a minister of religion the narrator—the Reverend Robert Russell —might profess to approve of this gradual oblivion, but one can sense an undertone of regret. Yarrow had been incomparably rich in ballads and legends. Now "there is no longer 'heard a lilting at the ewes' milking' or 'the tales at the farmer's ingle'."

For all that, the minstrel had long out-lived the warrior; his treasure was still there for the finding when Scott set forth on his ballad-reiving:

"He has rescued them; yet their publication in *The Border*

Minstrelsy was loss as well as gain,"—so Hogg's old mother had told Scott plainly.

"The spell that bound them was broken; and those relics of Border song, thus laid bare to the light of day, have, like the friendly and familiar spirits of Border superstition on being noticed with peculiar kindness, entirely disappeared, and that, in the consequence of the very effort made to preserve them". Hogg had played his part in this act of rescue that was part-destruction.

In Ettrick churchyard lies Thomas Boston, once minister of the parish, author of that formidable but fascinating classic of Calvinistic: theology "The Fourfold State". Another worthy of the past was Adam Scott of Tushielaw, commonly known as the King of Thieves, whom James V hanged one morning before breakfast, from an ash tree over his own gate.

The people of Ettrick were now closer in spirit to Mr. Boston than to Adam of Tushielaw, being "a reading people, well-informed on almost every subject. We can still trace among them the seeds of the gospel as sown here by the venerable Boston. They are quiet and inoffensive, and seem to cultivate all the dispositions which tend to peace and good agreement, to religion and morality."

They owed a great deal to a living benefactor, Lord Napier and Ettrick who had fought at Trafalgar and was now engaged in a war against poverty and neglect. He had been the agent for the improvement of roads in Yarrow and Ettrick, he had planted trees, he had introduced the profitable breed of Cheviot sheep.

He was living in the parish "and from his seat as a centre, life and, cultivation spreading and diffusing their happy influence all around us".

To return briefly into Roxburghshire, and to Hawick where, more than thirty years earlier, Scott had parted from the Wordsworths on their return south:—the scenery, if not magnificent "is nevertheless singularly interesting and beautiful" with the range of hills beyond "more remarkable for its gracefulness than for the wild and rugged features that are usually characteristic of mountain scenery. Teviot joined by Allen flowed through rich pastureland, "gliding with a solemn melody between the once festive halls of Branxholm and the massive peel of Goldielands". It was Douglas country; and in the fifteenth century Gavin Douglas,

Kelso Abbey and Cloister

poet in his own right, poet-translator of Virgil, priest and bishop had for a time been rector of the church. Hawick as seen by its minister, who was writing in the first years of Victoria's reign, in 1839, has plenty of history behind it, especially in the Border wars, and this was still apparent in its oldest buildings, made for shelter and defence with massive walls, on arches of whinstone. He found a like strength and ruggedness in the character of the people. "The truth is, the Border spirit, a spirit certainly more congenial with the usages of a ruder and less enlightened age than the present, is not altogether extinct." The folk of Hawick were jealous of their rights "keen and indefatigable in the working out of what they reckon to be their own interests . . . determined in asserting at all hazards what they deem to be essential to their own independence. Anything like a spirit of vassalage to any man, or to any class of men, hower elevated soever in rank, is what they cannot brook. . . . There are few places where less attention is paid to the ordinary distinctions of rank, or where all classes are more disposed to associate together on the footing of equality."

This is still true; Borderers are still a people at once proud, independent and loyal; it is a local, clan and family loyalty which has always been far from subservience. The rich man in his castle, the poor man at his gate are equal not only in the sight of heaven but as Borderers, fellow Scotts, Kerrs or Elliots. Hawick had perhaps more of the radical temper than most of the towns: "elements of character . . . which, if subject to the influence of religious principle and properly directed, might raise them to a very high point in the scale of moral and intellectual improvement" but might otherwise lead to excesses of political excitement (he was writing in the decade of the Chartists and of Parliamentary reforms) "which no right-minded man can contemplate with any other than a feeling of unqualified condemnation."

The town was already becoming industrial with the great majority of people employed in trade, the minority in agriculture, although this like the woollen manufacture had greatly improved and developed. The factories drew people in from other places.

The natives had marked characteristics and customs; among the latter "there is none certainly that is less deserving of notice, though none that is more characteristic, than that of distinguishing

Castle Pool on River Teviot at Kelso, ruins of
Roxburgh Castle in background

individuals by other than the names that properly belong to them". It was an old habit, made useful, almost necessary when so many bore the same surname; but these "fictitious designattions" or nicknames remained; some of the older inhabitants were hardly ever known by their real, legal and baptismal names, and the nicknames occurred even in the register of deaths. The minister, unfortunately for us, gives no examples.

Another custom, more solemn, concerned the dying. To the sickroom came family, kinsfolk and neighbours who sang together "with a low and solemn melody" one of the metrical psalms: the Twenty-Third, the Forty-Third or the Hundred and Eighteenth: psalms of trust in God up to and beyond the boundaries of this life, of humility and contrition. This was sung "while the soul of the dying person in passing into the world of spirits". And when the end had come, they sang another psalm, one of praise and triumph; some verses, often, of the Hundred and Seventh.

"That this practice has not originated from any species of superstitious feeling we are not prepared to affirm".

The Old Religion lingered long after it was officially deposed, openly condemned and rejected; traces of the former piety endured. In the solemnity of death, a memory and instinct, deeper than any conscious belief or feeling called for expression. These people would not have dared speak—perhaps not even thought—a word of prayer for the departed soul. But they did what they could, and their minister, obviously impressed yet uncertain of his own feelings adds: "It must be admitted that there is something in the service itself which is peculiarly impressive and solemnizing".

More cheerfully he writes of the Common Riding or Riding of the Marches. To this we shall return in an account of Hawick to-day.

One cannot leave these records of nineteenth-century Scotland and the Borders without a double regret: one, that Scott who made immortal so many Scottish types and personalities, who was a Borderer to the marrow and loved his country with such intimate knowledge and affection did not write more novels of that region—and of Edinburgh too. The other is that Scotland lacks a Victorian novelist presenting the Scottish scene. There were no major figures after Scott's death; two Victorians of great and versatile talent, George MacDonald and Margaret Oliphant, lived most of their writing lives in England. Both wrote about Scotland—MacDonald has some novels about his own north-east, Mrs. Oliphant of more than one region. The Borders, the old treasure-land of poetry and ballads had still a wealth of character; that this should not have been celebrated in fiction is one of the tragedies of our literature.

V

POETS AND MEN OF LETTERS

We find one of the largest, richest crops, both of intellect and imagination, in that limited district which stretches from the Pentlands to the Cheviots and the Solway.

—John Veitch

THE Borderers take to books, both to reading and writing them, as they do to fishing and sheep-farming, and as they once did to cattle-reiving. Professor Veitch, himself a Borderer, compared this region with Greece both in type of scenery and in achievement.

The scholar-parson, Thomas Somerville of Jedburgh, has already been mentioned. When his successor, John Purvis wrote his *Account* of the parish in 1834, this Father of the Church had been dead only four years; he was born in 1741, a middle-aged man when young Mr. Scott used to come about the manse on his visits to Jedburgh, during the Assizes, and during his journeys into the country to collect old ballads. Mrs. Somerville foretold his greatness, and she lived to enjoy not only *The Border Minstrelsy* but his own *Lay of the Last Minstrel* and *Marmion*. Scott's memory, for poems and stories and dialogue was remarkable; he entertained the minister and his wife with tales of the farms and cottages he had raided.

A country minister, in those days when committees were few and meetings infrequent could, even with the most devoted attention to his flock find ample time for study and for writing if he had a gift for it. George Ridpath of Stitchel had the passion for books and learning, and something of the gift; Thomas Somerville was a born scholar. Once settled in Jedburgh—in 1773—happily married, with a host of learned friends his thoughts and theirs turned to authorship:

"The subject . . . was the occasion of long and anxious delibera-
tion. Theology would have been most consonant to my taste
and habitual course of study, but was not likely to contribute
either to my profit or popularity."

So he turned to history, especially to political history, to the
period between the Restoration and the death of William of
Orange. For books he went to Edinburgh, to the Advocates'
Library and the College Library; some of the neighbouring
great houses, like Minto and Mellerstain had their own libraries
where he might browse and borrow; and he went to London,
to read in the British Museum, and indulge in a little worldly
pleasure as well. He enjoyed the theatre and saw Mrs. Siddons
as Lady Macbeth—"she outdid all description"—and as Rosalind
in which he found her less remarkable, her talent being for
tragedy. Having met John Wesley on the latter's visit to Scotland
he called on him to their mutual edification.

His book was published, very well reviewed but had no more
than a *succès d'estime*, of which he writes ruefully and disarmingly:

"The pride and self-conceit of authors naturally stimulate their
ingenuity in discovering every reason for the neglect of their
productions than that which is most commonly the true one."
His scholarly treatise was unlikely to be popular; and another
reason was the date of its publication, in 1792, when the horrors
of the French Revolution dominated the public mind. His next
work, on the reign of Queen Anne also had good notices, although none of the reviewers "expressed that decided approval
which they had bestowed on the former volume".

For later generations his best book is his memoir: *My Own
Life and Times* which he began in 1814 and which was published
after his death. It is admirable as a record; it recalls times past,
the period of his youth and early manhood in the eighteenth
century; and it is a self-portrait of a delightful personality, wise,
benign, tolerant. In an age of much bigotry he was altogether
in favour of the Catholic Emancipation Act. He enjoyed life and
wished others to enjoy it. In recalling the past and comparing it
with the present he deplores the decline in popular festivities
such as Valentine's Eve and Hallowe'en, regrets that games such
as handball, football, golf and bowls are less played, that there is
less of the simple but genial hospitality of his youth.

In material conditions life was harder then for the poor; one of the greatest changes for good he had seen was the improvement in farmhouses, once small and mean, now comfortable, and in agriculture and horticulture. The flower garden was a new and delightful thing "to the great increase of innocent enjoyment". In his youth the gardens of most country houses were chiefly for fruit and vegetables, and neither of these in great variety: only apples and pears, currants and gooseberries, potatoes and greens. Potatoes were not grown in open field before 1760 which made them dearer than meal as food. Meat was rarely eaten by the poor; bread, even in well-to-do households was more often of pease or barley meal than of wheaten flour; the latter was something of a delicacy. Tea had become cheap enough to be drunk in middle-class houses, in some only in the afternoon at a genteel party, in others for breakfast.

There were no circulating libraries then, in the country towns, but most people could and did read, and most cottages had a few books: *The Pilgrim's Progress* and Boston's *Fourfold State* among the most common.

But there was more popular merrymaking, and more observance of religion. That did not prevent a good deal of superstition.

"Not the populace only, but even many persons of good education believed in apparitions; haunted houses and haunted woods abounded, and innumerable ghost stories were in circulation in every parish, and implicitly believed by the bulk of the people. Belief in witchcraft was still more prevalent."

The age of reason might find expression in Edinburgh but on the Borders the old traditions had deep roots and from them grew strong, overshadowing trees. In Jedburgh, for a long time, the passing-bell was rung to announce a death; and between death and burial there was the "lykewake", the watching of the corpse; we have heard of this from the minister of Hawick. Prayers for the dead, the last sacraments of absolution, anointing and Holy Communion were utterly abhorred and rejected as Popish; but the old piety must have its expression, the solemnity of departure was recognised. A man's kindred and friends stayed with him even beyond the end.

There have been many scholars in the Borders, but the poets come first. The background makes poets, although in early poetry, in the ballads the modern romantic feeling for landscape, which

was at its height in Scott's day, is not apparent. These ballads
have "no tarrying sympathy with or full description of the
scenery. . . . The face of nature . . . as in itself an object of poetic
interest, did not strike the older minstrels. . . . Of nature as the
symbolism of human life and feeling we have no trace whatever"
—so John Veitch has observed. But such feeling is implicit,
hidden deep in the poetry, it is part of the source. The ballads
have an awareness of the reality beyond appearances.

And in the ballads the very names have music and magic.
With Scott we come into the romantic consciousness of scenery.
It would be easy to make a Book of the Borders from his poems,
not, certainly, a guide to travellers in the matters of roads,
mileage and direction, but a poetic map. His friend John Leyden,
a scholar whose range and profundity of learning would, in an
earlier age, have been ascribed to wizardry, was also a poet, no
genius but with a talent for fluent narrative and description.
Recollections in Verse might describe his long poem *Scenes of
Infancy*. It is, at its best, evocative.

Leyden, born in 1775, was the son of poor parents; his father
was grieve or farm-manager for a more prosperous relation.
They lived in a lonely cottage at Henlawshiel, under Rubislaw.
The boy was taught to read by his grandmother, and he devoured
all the books he could lay hands on: the Bible, poetry, stories of
Wallace and Bruce, The Arabian Nights (that exotic treasury
often appeared in Scottish homes). Moreover, he was fed on
living literature.

"A Border peasant at that time lived in an atmosphere of romantic tradition and exciting ballad" as an early biographer, W. W.
Tulloch wrote in his Introduction to Leyden's poem.

Young John walked many miles to school at Kirkton, and had
tuition besides from the minister of Denholm, in Latin and
Greek. (The hidden contribution of many a parish minister and
schoolmaster to Scottish scholarship has not been fully valued.)
This good man had his reward when his pupil acquired enough
of the classics to pass into Edinburgh University; there he stayed
for five or six years, living no doubt on oatmeal and herring
like many another lad of parts and poverty, swallowing vast
quantities of learning. He was known both for his erudition and
his uncouthness. His particular talent, almost genius was for
languages; to his Latin and Greek he added French, Italian,

Spanish, German and Icelandic, with Hebrew and other Oriental languages for good measure. At home in the long vacation, from Easter till October, he used to study in the old parish church of Cavers which was said to be haunted. This suited him very well; when interrupted by inquisitive locals, he staged an apparition of the devil, scared off the intruders and was left in peace.

His poems in *The Edinburgh Magazine*, some original, some translations from the Greek, were noticed by Scott; they met in 1794, when Leyden began to help in collecting material for *The Border Minstrelsy*. Meanwhile he went on writing; he tutored, to earn his keep, he tried but failed to be appointed to a church. The article on him in *The Dictionary of National Biography* says, mildly and credibly, that "his pulpit appearances were not successful". His biographer, however, thought that had he waited he would have been given the charge of Duddingston-where, in 1805, came another remarkable cleric, one of the most delightful in the annals of the kirk, John Thomson, the artist-minister.

Leyden changed course entirely. Having qualified, after six months, in medicine and surgery, he went out to India, in 1803, as assistant-surgeon in Madras. There he prospered; his gift for languages being, as Dominie Sampson, a kindred spirit, would say, prodigious, he became professor of Hindustani in Calcutta in 1805; he also held a judgeship and commissionership, was appointed Assay-Master of the Mint in Calcutta, and went as consultant geologist, naturalist and surgeon with the Commissioners into the Province of Mysore. It is a far cry from the cottage under Rubislaw and the old kirk of Cavers. This fantastically brilliant career ended, after its rapidity, in 1811 when, still in his thirties, Leyden died of a fever picked up on his last expedition, to Java, with Lord Minto.

"No more attentive ear than his ever listened to the music of those viewless harps, and in his poetry and ballads we may hear its echoes." The echoes may be faint, but the enchantment is caught at times. In his poem Leyden recalls Merlin: "the magic harp of ancient Teviotdale" and the fighting ballads:

> I see the combat through the mist of years,
> When Scott and Douglas led the Border spears.

Much of his poetry is *genre* painting in verse, perhaps a Nasmyth interior:

> Still to the surly strain of martial deeds,
> In cadence soft, the dirge of love succeeds,
> With tales of ghosts that haunt unhallowed ground;
> While, narrowing still, the circle closes round
> Till, shrinking pale from nameless shapes of fear,
> Each peasant starts his neighbour's voice to hear.

His verse is landscape-painting too:

> Dark Ruberslaw, that lifts his head sublime,
> Ragged and hoary with the mists of time!
> On his broad misty front the giant wears
> The horrid furrows of ten thousand years.

Of the confluence of little waters in Teviot and her confluence with Tweed at Kelso, he writes that that lovely valley, lovely at all times is loveliest

> ... At midnight's shadowy reign
> When liquid silver floods the moonlight plain,
> And lawns and fields and woods of varying hue
> Drink the wan lustre and the pearly dew;
> While the still landscape, more than noontide bright,
> Glistens with mellow tints of fairy light.

The magic is intensified:

> By every thorn along the woodland damp
> The tiny glow-worm lights her emerald lamp;
> Like the shot-star whose yet unquenched light
> Studs with faint gleam the raven-vest of night,
> The fairy ring-dance now round Eildon-tree
> Moves to wild strains of elfin minstrelsy.

Recalling the story of Thomas the Rhymer—"dire to the minstrel was the fairy's boon" he tells how a Border shepherd was once led into the heart of the Eildons by one whom he discovered to be Thomas himself, and there saw Arthur's knights awaiting the return of their King from the place where he had gone.

Leyden's boyhood, remembered in these "Scenes of Infancy"

had not, however, been given wholly to books and legends; he can describe with zest all the fun of the fair:

> The merry bustle and the mixed uproar
> Where every face a jovial aspect wore;

the pedlars with their enticements:

> glittering trinkets in alluring rows . . .
> Proud o'er the gazing group his form to rear,
> Bawls from his cart the vagrant auctioneer;
> While many an oft-repeated tale he tells,
> And jokes adapted to the wares he sells.

James Hogg had the same background as Leyden: son of a poor sheep-farmer whose farm failed, and young James had to go to the herding when he was only seven. He went herding in summer, his wages being a pair of shoes and a ewe-lamb, and in winter he went to school. Born at Ettrickhall in 1770 he was of Border stock on both sides, his mother a Laidlaw. At fifteen he went as shepherd to another Laidlaw, the sheep-farmer of Blackhouse in Yarrow, whose son Will became his friend; the same Will was to be Scott's faithful servant and friend to his life's end. Hogg began to read voraciously, like Leyden, though his was not the scholar's mind; his knowledge of Border tales and ballads, drawn from his mother, was known to the Laidlaws and when Scott called at Blackhouse one day in 1801 Hogg was summoned to meet him: "I'm thinkin' it's the Shirra and some of his gang," said the messenger.

The gang which included Leyden was increased by Hogg and by young Laidlaw, then about twenty-one; they rode by Douglas Burn to Whitehope, where Laidlaw's uncle lived; on by St. Mary's Loch which was Scott's first sight of that lovely water, and there Will gave them the ballad of "Auld Maitland", remembering long afterwards Leyden's wild enthusiasm. It is said that in the reign of James V gold was found about Douglas Burn. The Shirra and his gang found much fine gold of poetry and of friendship; Scott met Hogg's mother and was reproved for polishing and publishing the poems in *The Border Minstrelsy*: "They were made for singin' and no' for readin'; but ye hae broken the charm noo, and they'll never be sung mair."

Hogg was one of the company at supper when the discussion,

which so puzzled and amused Scott broke out anent long sheep and short sheep; recognising this dialogue in the first chapter of *The Black Dwarf* he knew the authorship of the novel.

The friendship with Scott endured, though it must often have tried Scott's patience. Hogg had no small sense of his own value and was never sensitive about intrusion. One can imagine Mrs. Scott's private comments after some of his visits. Another friendship was with Professor John Wilson (Christopher North) with whom the Ettrick Shepherd, as Hogg came to be called, spent the *Noctes Ambrosianae*—the Nights at Ambrose's Tavern—which still make good reading. The publication in 1813 of his long poem *The Queen's Wake* brought him fame and a fair success. As a poet he attained moments of pure magic, especially in "Kilmeny" the story of the girl who went—not into Elfhame but to a holier place, some lost Paradise:

> Where the cock never crew,
> Where the rain never fell, and the wind never blew . . .
> A land where sin had never been;
> A land of love and a land of light,
> Withouten sun or moon or light . . .
> The land of vision, it would seem,
> A still, an everlasting dream.

The magic of the Borders has been transmuted into holiness. Kilmeny has gone not, like Thomas the Rhymer, into perilous enchantment but into peace and security, whence she returns bringing peace with her that touches every creature she meets. But like True Thomas she cannot remain in this world; she is drawn away not by bidding of the Fairy Queen but by spiritual nostalgia. This world of ours

> Wasna her hame, and she couldna remain;
> She left this world of sorrow and pain,
> And returned to the land of thought again.

The Ettrick Shepherd remained a shepherd; thanks to Scott's advocacy he was given, by the Duke of Buccleugh, at a nominal rent, the farm of Altrive. He married, at the age of fifty. A second farm, Mount Benger, was unsuccessful and he retired to Altrive where he was happy. When Scott invited him to London, for the Coronation of George IV, he declined; it would mean missing St. Boswell's Fair. His friend and fellow-poet Allan

Cunningham approved. What had London to offer more than Altrive?

"He has the finest trout in Yarrow, the finest sheep on the braes, the finest grouse on the hills, and besides, he as good as keeps a small still."

Hogg outlived Scott by three years, writing a Memoir of him in *Domestic Manners of Sir Walter Scott*. A monument to him stands by St. Mary's Loch.

As for Will Laidlaw he has left one good poem: "Lucy's Flittin'," but his claim to remembrance outmeasures that modest achievement. Scott had no better helper, no more devoted friend. Will Laidlaw is truly one of the makers of Abbotsford. On Scott's return from Italy, his last home-coming, old beyond his years, broken and nearly finished he roused from his torpor for a moment:

Ha! Willie Laidlaw! O man, how often have I thought of you!

John Veitch who praised the scholars and poets of the Borders was no mean scholar himself, hardly less than Leyden though not so richly eccentric. He was born within Scott's lifetime, in 1829, in Peebles, the son of a sergeant of Wellington's army; went to school in the town, then to Edinburgh University at sixteen which was not an unusually youthful age at that period, and heard the lectures of William Edmonstoune Aytoun, himself a poet, of John Wilson (Christopher North) whose grasp of his official subject, philosophy, was not of the strongest, and that undoubted scholar Sir William Hamilton to whom he became assistant in the department of Logic and Metaphysics. In 1860 Veitch was appointed to the Chair of Logic, Rhetoric and Metaphysics in St. Andrews; in 1864 he moved to Glasgow University where he stayed for the thirty years of life that remained to him. Life in those days, for a professor, had ample leisure for study in his own subject or his hobbies; there was the long vacation between Easter and October which was spent in his own house in Peebles, on the borders of the true Scott country. The fruit of those vacations was in his essays and poems.

Like the Ettrick Shepherd and many another lad he owed much to his mother, if not in book-learning certainly in folk-lore and living memories. In his *Border Essays* he writes of Manor Valley in Peeblesshire, as "proportioned, restrained and complete as a Greek temple, supremely perfect and lovable" and with "a mysterious power of suggestion". Magic lay around it. In this valley had lived David Ritchie, translated and immortalised by Scott as Elshender the Black Dwarf, known locally, from his deformity, as Bowed Davie. Veitch's mother had seen him in her girlhood, and she had a tale of an old woman who encountered him one day when she was herding the cattle:

"I saw the tap of a lang stick, coming up as it were ahint the dyke, and there was nae heid ava, and naebody to be seen, juist a lang stick, too'ering ower the dyke, and I was feared. I was juist gaun to rin hame and leave the kye, when a wee bit bodie wi' the lang stick began to sprachle [scramble] ower the dyke. . . . He said naething as he gaed by me, but juist gied a queer kind o' glower."

Davie was not malignant, was, indeed, a sociable creature: "He was an awfu' bodie to crack [talk] . . . his tongue gaed like the clapper o' a mill. . . . We were a' fond o' his cracks . . . he tel't us about witches and warlocks." But the woman ended: "I wouldna hae putten my haun on his shouther for a' the world".

With this real character was linked one of legend: the Brown Man of the moors, a Border faun or Pan: "Lord of all the harmless creatures, the red deer, and peewit, whaup and grouse, and black game and speeding mountain deer. They were his subjects and his creatures, and it was his duty and privilege to watch over them." With this legend was linked that of a Black Dwarf who, though not malignant, would punish farmers and shepherds for any injury done to the sheep and cattle, and who was an apparition of ill omen: "When he showed himself, it was a prophecy of evils coming on the land."

Scott used this tradition in his story. He makes the grand-dame of Heugh-foot tell of the Black Dwarf's having been seen in the year of Marston Moor, of the war of Montrose and the battle of Dunbar, and that of Bothwell Brig: "O bairns, he's never permitted but in an ill time".

And Scott met the real Davie. In 1792, on his way to the Lake District—the tour on which he met his future wife, Charlotte—he stayed with his friend Adam Fergusson at Hallyards, and was taken up the Manor valley to Davie's cottage. There was a deep mutual impression.

"Hae ye ony poo'er?" Davie asked Scott, meaning magic
power. Scott disavowed it. As he was leaving, a black cat like
a familiar spirit appeared, and Davie pronounced: "He has
poo'er; aye, *he* has poo'er."

Among the ladies of the Borders are two who are remembered
by a song. One may claim, besides, to have been Scott's first
love. The love of his heart briefly met, never forgotten was
Williamina Stuart Belsches who married his friend Sir William
Forbes; there was a lass in Kelso, too, named Jessie with whom
the boy Walter corresponded for a little after his return to
Edinburgh. This other, much older love was Mrs. Cockburn, his
senior by nearly sixty years; she was born Alison Rutherford,
cousin in some degree to Scott's mother, and her home was the
old house of Fairnilee. This had been Ker property and passed
to the Rutherfords on the marriage of Alison Ker to Robert
Rutherford, about 1700; our Alison was their daughter. All her
life she loved her old home, Tweedside and all the Borderland:

"I can this minute figure myself," she wrote, as an old lady,
to her friend Dr. Douglas of Galashiels (from whom Scott was
to buy Clarty Hole and make it Abbotsford) "running fast as a
greyhound on a hot, summer day, to have the pleasure of plung-
ing into Tweed. I see myself made up like a ball, with my feet
wrapt in my petticoat, on the declivity of the hill at Fairnilee,
letting myself roll to the bottom, with infinite delight."

It was to Dr. Douglas she wrote, in 1777, her account of
calling on Mrs. Scott at 25 George Square and meeting "the most
extraordinary genius of a boy I ever saw": the six-year old
Walter. He returned her admiration, telling his aunt that night
that he liked that lady: "I think she is a virtuoso like myself."

Mrs. Cockburn was one of the great ladies of Edinburgh in
the golden age of the eighteenth century when wit, intelligence,
character and a long pedigree were valued far above wealth,
and a *salon* to match any in Paris could be maintained in a modest
parlour with tea or a frugal supper to fortify the guests. She was
comely as well as clever, and kind as she was comely. Her guests
included the most brilliant men in Edinburgh of that day, David
Hume, Lord Monboddo among them; Scott was a young man,
not yet come to fame, when she died in 1794, but she, before
anyone else, had discerned his quality.

She wrote the song: "I've seen the smiling of Fortune beguiling" which is still sung to the tune of "The Floo'ers o' the Forest". There is a tradition, which has been discredited, that she wrote it at the request of a gentleman visiting Fairnilee, who had heard the tune played by a shepherd on his whistle. Scott, in the third volume of his *Border Minstrelsy* gives it with a more material and realistic derivation; that she wrote it after the financial disaster which ruined seven Selkirk lairds together. He added the affectionate tribute:

"Even at an age advanced beyond the usual bounds of humanity, she retained a play of imagination and an activity of intellect which must have been attractive and delightful in youth, but was almost preternatural at her period of life. Her active benevolence, keeping pace with her genius, rendered her equally an object of love and admiration." He suggests that the song may refer also to the depopulation of Ettrick Forest.

In the same volume he gives the other, better known, oftener sung words: "I've heard them liltin' at our ewe-milkin'" with their direct and poignant memory of Flodden, their realistic evocation of a countryside bereft of young manhood. In this song "composed many years ago, by a lady in Roxburghshire," Scott found "the manner of the ancient minstrels is so happily imitated that it required the most positive evidence to covince the Editor that the song was of modern date".

The lady was Jean Elliot, daughter of Sir Gilbert Elliot the second baronet of Minto in Teviotdale, ancestor of the Earls of Minto. The story is that her brother Gilbert wagered a pair of gloves to a set of ribbons on her writing such a poem. She won. When published anonymously the song was accepted by many readers as geniunely old, so haunting and true is it in feeling and expression. Mrs. Cockburn's is reflective, a drawing-room elegy; Jean Elliot's as factual as any of the old ballads. But both have beauty. Mrs. Cockburn mentions her poem once, in a letter to Dr. Douglas:

"I hate print, and though I have been sung at Wells to the Flowers of the Forest, I was never in print that any but a street singer could decipher."—By "Wells" she means the genteel health resorts of Moffat and St. Ronans or Innerleithen where people went to drink the waters and enjoy concerts and assemblies. The tune is very old, even if the story of the shepherd and his whistle is a myth.

A third poetess of the Borders is Lady John Scott whose life nearly spanned the century, from 1810 till 1900; she was born Alicia Spottiswoode. Among her delightful songs are a version of "Annie Laurie", and one, most fitting for this account of the Borders, called "Ettrick"; a song of youth and love, age and inevitable sorrow:

> When we first rade down Ettrick,
> Our bridles were ringing, our hearts were dancing,
> The waters were singing, the sun was glancing. . . .
>
> . . . When we next rade down Ettrick,
> The day was dying, the wild birds calling,
> The wind was sighing, the leaves were falling. . . .
>
> . . . When I last rade down Ettrick,
> The winds were shifting, the storm was waking,
> The snow was drifting, my heart was aching,
> For we never again were to ride thegither
> In sun or in storm on the mountain heather.

The lyric and elegiac note, as old almost as the land and the rivers, is heard in modern as in the ancient poetry of the Borders.

Night view of Galashiels War Memorial

VI

VICTORIAN BORDERERS:
BOYHOOD ON THE BORDERS

Gie me a Border burn
That canna rin without a turn.
—J. B. Selkirk

There's mony a water, great or sma',
  Gaes singing in his siller tune
Through glen and heugh, and hope and shaw,
  Beneath the sunlicht or the moon;
But set us in oor fishing-shoon
  Between the Caddon-burn and Peel,
And syne we'll cross the heather broun
  By fair Tweedside, at Ashiestiel.
                           —Andrew Lang

IN THE year Scott died, 1832, a boy was born in Galashiels, over
the river who was to love the Borders as dearly, and was to continue, in his own modest and endearing way, the tradition of
Border bard. He was John Buchan Brown, who wrote under
the pen-name of J. B. Selkirk. His parents moved to Selkirk
when he was very small and he went to school there; he could
not become a Souter o' Selkirk, for to be that a man must be a
native, but he was, in the good Scots word, thirled to the town
from which he took his name as poet.

As a young man he went into his father's woollen manufactory, and like many another, lived a double life of the utmost
virtue: at once business man and poet, lover of books and
history, of all that concerned the Borders. His first volume of
verse was published in 1869; he lived into the new century,
dying in 1905.

The best of his poems have the authentic, traditional quality,
the power of evocation, the singing note, the homeliness with

97

Early summer in Tweeddale, St. Boswell's
Earlston

dignity. They speak the true Border Scots, with the magic of names in them. Perhaps his best-known is the letter in verse, "Homeward Mail", written by an emigrant in Canada to his friend Tam at home: a song of exile none the less poignant for its homeliness. At the first service held by the little Scottish community overseas, in the hall used as a church, they sing the Old Hundredth:

> The like o't no' been ken'd for praise
> In Ettrick Kirk since Boston's days.

This exile pined for home, although he had good friends near him, Borderers all:

> There's Gibbie Elliot, Kinmont Bob . . .
> There's Telfer, Douglas, Learmont, Scott . . .

but Canada was a poor-looking place compared with the Borders. He fell sick; the doctor

> A man respeckit near and far,
> His grannie was a Sprouston Ker

knew, by his own Border blood, what ailed his patient:

> My trouble's been—the greater pairt—
> A rush of Ettrick to the hairt.

And then come the memories:

> Ah, Tam! gie me a Border burn
> That canna rin without a turn

—that dives underground for a length, then

> Out again, the loupin' limmer,
> Comes dancin' doun through shine and shimmer . . .
> Then on its way it gies a ca'
> At Fauldhope, Aikwood, Carterha',
> Where fairy-fettered young Tam Lane
> Through love's great power was freed again

—and so on to the meeting of waters and the deep pool:

> I've fish't it often as a callant,
> Wi' muckle zeal and little talent.

There is no remedy for this sick exile but return to the Borders and their rivers.

There is also the nostalgia for the past, when the old man in "Looking Back on Yarrow" recalls the peaceful days of his youth. He finds his young contemporaries ignorant of the old speech and the old tunes—and this was a Victorian poem! There is prosperity enough, Jock dressing like the laird, his wife Kirsty "just as braw" and if she would but hold her tongue might pass for a lady! Already the tourists are swarming:

> They've gliffed awa' the fairies, [frightened]
> Sin' a' the warld maun gang
> An' picnic at St. Mary's.

They would seem small and peaceful throngs to us, nowadays, coming in horse-drawn vehicles, at perhaps twelve miles an hour. Borderers still enjoy excursions. The "Mystery Tour" is popular in summer among the women's guilds and clubs in the towns. You pays your money but you don't take your choice of route; the bus takes you where the driver and possibly the club secretary choose. And still there are old people who, in true Border accents with good Scots words deplore the passing of the native speech; pronounce the modern young to be restless, extravagant, corrupted by American films, television and other vanities. But it would be rash to offer most old folk the gift of "the telly" if you did not want it to be accepted.

The man "Looking Back on Yarrow" could remember the days when

> Nae wheel but on a barrow,
> And Dr. Russell's gig
> Was ever seen on Yarrow.

And now—cars and bicycles have long since replaced the gig and cart. Every farm has its tractor and manifold machinery. Yet Yarrow and all the Border country keep the ancient beauty and peace.

One of J. B. Selkirk's poems recalls Flodden, in words given to a Border Widow. Like Jean Elliot's song it holds the undying poignancy.

But Flodden is remembered by many who never rhymed one word with another. They have long memories in the Borders. Selkirk still enacts a dramatic memorial of that day of dolour.

Another Victorian could rightly claim to be a Souter of

Selkirk: Andrew Lang, who was born there in 1844, of good Border stock going back many generations. He could claim some drops of the blood of Scott of Harden. His father was a lawyer and Town Clerk—"a just-living man for a country lawyer" in Scott's phrase; his mother was a sister of that notable classical scholar, William Sellar, Professor of Humanity in Edinburgh University. There was scholarship in his blood, with such a diversity of other gifts that he has been honoured less than he deserves. Andrew Lang cannot be neatly classified; but this richness and diversity show him to be a true Borderer.

His was a happy childhood, let loose among books and in the enchanted countryside. Something of it he has told directly in his *Angling Sketches* and his *Adventures Among Books*; his recent biographer, Roger Lancelyn Green suggests that in the childhood of Randal and Jean in his story: *The Gold of Fairnilee* his own Victorian boyhood is recalled, or reflected as in a magic mirror.

"Legends float about the whole countryside", the editor, T. Craig Brown, of Mrs. Cockburn's Letters, said of her old home of Fairnilee set above Tweed, looking over the Yair, close to the ancient camp of the Rink and to Catrail, "that mysterious roadway". Andrew Lang caught the magic in a tale which unites the old legends of fairyland with the thrill of treasure-trove. His Fairnilee belongs to the Kers and the laird is slain at Flodden. His only child, Randal, and his adopted sister Jean grow up in the country with just such country pleasures as Lang himself and his brothers and sisters knew more than three hundred years later. They go fishing in Caddon Burn and Burn of Peel, act tournaments with helmets of green rushes and spears of bulrushes; listen to old tales from their nurse.

"In summer they were always on the hills and by the burnside. You cannot think, if you have not tried, what pleasant company a burn is. It comes out of the deep, black wells in the moss, far away on the tops of the hills where the sheep feed, and the fox peers from his hole, and the ravens breed in the crags. The burn flows down from the lonely places, cutting a way between steep green banks, tumbling in white waterfalls over rocks, and lying in deep, black pools below the waterfalls. At every turn it does something new, and plays a fresh game with its brown waters. The white pebbles in the water look like gold."

It is a perfect description of a Border burn "that canna rin without a turn", of the gleam and glitter of the Border landscape so intricately interwoven with living water.

The children build a dam of stone and turf, then break it to let the water stream down in a flood, or "hurly-gush" which is a better word. In winter they slide on the frozen pools; and they follow with the sheep-dog the track of wild creatures in the snow. Andrew and his brothers must have done this too; he shows the marks on a page of his book: the rabbit's, the hare's, "but the fox's is just as if you had pushed a piece of wood through the snow". They put out porridge for the grouse and black-cock sheltering in the trees. Swans escaping from the frozen hill-lochs float on the open reaches of Tweed.

"It was pleasant to be a boy then in the north"—pleasant to be a boy there three hundred years and more later, and the young Langs has, besides, the pleasure of books. For Randal and Jean there were fireside tales told by their nurse, old Nancy, who may be a portrait of the Langs' own nurse. The picture of the long dark nights of winter, by the fire, is Victorian. Nurse spins as she talks and her shadow sometimes, to Jean's imagination looks like that of a fairy-woman at a magic spinning-wheel; for her stories are most often of elves and fairies.

Perhaps from evenings like those in the nursery of the Town Clerk's house in Selkirk came much of the treasure in the many-coloured Fairy Books Lang was to edit. Other tales are of buried treasure: if you believed her, there was hardly an old stone on the hillside but had gold under it. The sheep feeding on Eildon had yellow teeth because there was gold under the grass; and there was gold at Fairnilee:

> Atween the wet ground and the dry
> The gold of Fairnilee doth lie;

or, as another rhyme puts it more precisely:

> Between the Camp o' Rink
> And Tweed water clear,
> Lie nine kings' ransoms,
> For nine hundred year.

The children believe it; and as there is a wishing well not far away, on a hilltop between Tweed and Yarrow they go there to wish. It brings peril to Randal; he is lured away, like Thomas the Rhymer, for seven long years. Then, like Tam Linn he is rescued and brought back by brave Jean. During his absence things have gone badly; there has been a long, bitter winter—such as can come often to the Borders—with famine following; more than ever is the gold of Fairnilee needed. Randal has brought one treasure back from faery; a tiny bottle of water which, rubbed on the eyes, gives clear sight. It gives him the sight of where the treasure lies on the ground above Catrail, the old dry ditch or roadway between Tweed and the hill— "Nobody knows who made it or why", with Camp of Rink above it and its tall standing stones. And here the gold is found with much more treasure: a kettle full of golden coins, a box filled with bars of gold, cups of silver and gold and fine glass, a golden figure of Fortune: Roman treasure hidden these nine hundred years and more, and it brings comfort, prosperity and luck to Fairnilee and all the country round about. Randal marries Jean, their children play by the river as they did, and hear the same tales and songs; they die on the same day and are buried in Dryburgh. "The Tweed goes murmuring past their grave, and the grave of Sir Walter Scott."

If Andrew Lang found no buried gold at Fairnilee or anywhere else, he had, all his life a rich treasure of poetry and legends, of old books; and the country gold of days of sport by river and hill. His was such a boyhood as Scott would have loved had it not been for his lameness. His favourite sport was fishing, though looking back from his middle years he admits to being "devoted to fishing rather than the catching of fish", to having "been born an angler" but born under an unlucky star; fishing, like the man in J. B. Selkirk's poem, "Wi' muckle zeal and little talent". One of his earliest memories was of fishing, with a bent pin, for minnows "or 'baggies' as we called them" along with some playmates, in Ettrick. But no minnows were caught.

His younger brother once asked him: "What do *you* do in sermon time? Mind you don't tell. I tell stories to myself about catching trout". Andrew made a like confession. "Even so, I drove the sermon by; and I have not 'told' till now."

He and his brothers were taken upstream, to Ladhope on Yarrow, where he caught a troutling, his brother a good half-pounder, rousing envy in Andrew's heart. "It was worth while to be a boy then in the south of Scotland." Even then, in the 1850s, local anglers complained that the water was "owre sair fished". Andrew thought that in the days before "the hills were drained, before the manufacturing towns were so populous, before pollution, netting, dynamiting, poisoning" and other modern horrors, "the Border must have been the angler's paradise. Still, it was not bad when we were boys."

The towns have grown still more—but still there is good fishing on Tweed, Ettrick and Yarrow; no doubt with reflections on the part of anglers on the paradisal state of the rivers and country a century ago.

There was a trout pool at Lindean, and a fine stretch of water from there to the confluence of Ettrick with Tweed; there was sea-trout in Tweed itself; in the pool between Ashestiel and Gleddis Well there was salmon. Scott and Hogg used to spear salmon there. Lang quotes a phrase from Franck, a contemporary of Izaak Walton, about "the glittering and resolute stream of Tweed".

Glittering and resolute, it made a worthy antagonist in the sport; yet even without the thrill of tension it was delightful and alluring:

"The steep banks, beautifully wooded, and in spring one mass of primroses, are crowned here and there, with ruined Border towers. . . . Thirty years ago [he was writing in 1891] the burns that feed St. Mary's Loch were almost unfished, and rare sport we had in them as boys, staying at Tibbie Shiel's famous cottage, and sleeping in her box-beds where so often the Ettrick Shepherd and Christopher North have lain, after copious toddy."

Like J. B. Selkirk he laments the invasion by tourist: "Yarrow is only the old Yarrow in winter. Ages and revolutions must pass before the ancient peace returns".

But the peace is still there to be found.

"The Aill near Sinton and Ashkirk was a delightful trout-stream. . . . Nowhere on the Borders were trout more numerous, better fed, and more easily beguiled. . . . Memory, which has lost so much, and would gladly lose so much more, brings vividly back the golden summer evenings by Tweedside, when the trout began to plash in the stillness, brings back the long, lounging solitary days beneath the woods of Ashestiel, days so lonely that they sometimes, in the end, begat a superstitious eeriness. One seemed forsaken in an enchanted world."

He recalls "the alternate pool and stream" of Border waters where

> The triple pride
> Of Eildon looks over Strathclyde

and where the fisherman casts for salmon "hard by the wizard's grave", Merlin's, at Drummelzier. Many rivers are beloved but dearest of all are Ettrick and Tweed. "In any river you knew of yore, you can find the Fountains of Youth."

Becoming realistic and rueful he admits that a bad day's fishing does not inspire poetic reflections:

"After all that bad luck, one is not in the vein for legendary lore, nor memories of boyhood, nor poetry or sunsets. I do not believe that one ever thinks of the landscape or of anything else, while there is a chance for a fish, and no abundance of local romance can atone for an empty creel."

Yet he ends with devotion:

He who has given his heart to Tweed . . . will never change his love".

It was indeed good to be a boy in that valley, "to fish the waters haunted by old legends, musical with old songs . . . the golden summer evenings by Tweedside . . . the long solitary days beneath the woods of Ashestiel. . . . One seemed forsaken in a supernatural world; one might see the two white fairy deer flit by, bringing to us, as to Thomas the Rhymer, the tidings that we must back to Fairyland."

Books and fishing, adventures in literature and on the river were closely linked. His angling, indeed, led to one discovery among books. He learned to read at the age of four and from the first was omnivorous. One afternoon he and his brothers were taken to the cottage of the local carpenter who made their fishing-rods. In one of the few books lying on a shelf Andrew found these lines:

> The Baron of Smailholme rose with day
> And spurred his charger on.

It was his introduction to Sir Walter Scott. He became so engrossed in the poem as to take less than a normal interest in the home-baked scones and honey provided for tea.

"Scott is not an author like any other, but our earliest friend in letters. . . . Scott peopled for us the rivers and burnsides with his reivers; the Fairy Queen came out of Eildon Hill and haunted Carterhaugh."

In *Adventures Among Books* he records that "there was usually a little volume of Scott in one's pocket, in company with the miscellaneous collection of a boy's treasures. Scott certainly took his fairy folk seriously. . . . After this kind of introduction to Sir Walter, after learning one's first lessons in history from *The Tales of a Grandfather* nobody, one hopes, can criticise him in cold blood."

From Selkirk Grammar School Andrew went, at the age of ten, to Edinburgh Academy—a school which Scott had helped to found. Life in the house of the old relation with whom he stayed was dull, until he found the Waverley Novels. "The rest is transport. . . . For a year I was a young hermit, living with Scott in the 'Waverleys' and *The Border Minstrelsy*." His school work was adequately done; that saved trouble; but his absorption in romance led to his being forbidden novels for a time. On discovering that his obedience was tempered by reading *Don Juan* his parents lifted the ban.

His scholarly mind developed; at seventeen he went to St. Andrews University, then, for a session to Glasgow where he won the Snell Exhibition in Classics, and to Oxford which he loved only second to Tweedside.

Oxford, and, after his marriage London made the background of his maturity and professional life as man of letters. In later years he came back to Scotland, to St. Andrews. His writing was of infinite variety; in his Prefaces to the Border Edition of the Waverley Novels, published in 1893–1894 he expresses his two loves—of Scott and of the Borders. The magic which caught him in boyhood was never broken; in memory he returned to the hills and waters of Tweedside.

VII

THE TWEED TOWNS

Sing, my bonny, harmless sheep
That feed upon the mountains steep,
Bleating sweetly as ye go
Through the winter's frost and snow;

Hart and hind and fallow deer
Not by half as useful are;
Frae king to him that hauds the plough,
All are obliged to Tarry Woo'.

Tarry Woo' is ill to spin,
Card it weel ere ye begin,
When 'tis carded, row'd and spun
Then the wark is halfling done,

But when woven, drest and clean
It may be cleading for a queen.

So RUNS the song of Galashiels, given by T. Craig Brown, a Selkirk man, in his *History of Selkirkshire* or *Chronicles of Ettrick
Forest*, published some eighty years ago. The tarry woo' or
wool, duly carded, rolled and spun, washed and dressed has
made clothing for queens of fashion. The Border towns still
produce the warm, hard-wearing tweeds needed for hard work
and a hard climate, but they have learned also to make a material
almost as soft and fine as velvet and silk, as rich and subtle in
colour as a queen could desire.

The monks had begun the wool-trade and kings continued
to favour it. In 1428 James I came into the business, exporting
wool from the crown pastures. So much, indeed was sent abroad
that a little later the Scots Parliament tried to develop the home
use and treatment of wool by inviting Flemish weavers to come
over and teach the Scots their skill—hence the name of Fleming.

In 1581 there is record of two waulking or fulling mills in Galashiels, and from that date onward, weaving developed rapidly.

During the Civil War weavers were exempt from military service and war taxation; these privileges were continued by Cromwell and by Charles II, the latter giving masters of the industry the power to seize beggars and vagabonds and compel them to learn weaving. The Weavers' Incorporation was founded in 1666. The final privilege was the rescinding by Parliament of the law compelling everyone to be buried in a linen shroud, and substituting wool for the dead, as for the living. Grants were made by successive monarchs, and all was set for the beginning of the modern tweed trade round about 1830.

Scott's share in this has been mentioned. Craig Brown gives other stories of tweed's rise to fashion, all of them good and probably true. One is that the thick tweed woven in Jedburgh was much worn by Lord Lothian and by Scott of Harden, especially for fishing; other fishermen discovered its water-resistant quality and so began the demand for sports wear. Cloaks in shepherd's plaid had long been worn; trousers in the same pattern became fashionable (here Scott comes into the story); by happy accident some wool was dyed brown instead of white, so a brown and black pattern was achieved, and then other mixtures. The next step was the import of wool finer than the Border sheep could supply, much of it from Australia where many Borderers had emigrated and acquired large sheep farms. And thus, gradually, came the "cleading for a queen" or as Craig Brown puts it more practically, wool became "suitable either for the rough coat of the shepherd roaming over the cold hills of Scotland, or for the cool and airy vestment of the planter under tropical sun".

Another aid to development was of course machinery, first imported from Yorkshire to make the process of spinning and weaving quicker, and produce larger quantities and more varied patterns and textures. Towards the end of the eighteenth century the weaving of flannel was begun by George Mercer.

Tweed in its intricacy of colour and pattern is a true symbol of the Borders, both of the landscape with its diversity of hill and wood, pasture and river, grandeur and peacefulness, and of its history in which past and present are inextricably interwoven.

The growth of the trade, too, has not been entirely due to merchants and craftsmen though theirs is the greater part. Scott, Lord Lothian and others gave it impetus; and that good cleric Dr. Douglas of Galashiels, friend of Mrs. Cockburn, owner of the house and land which became Abbotsford, was one of its chief benefactors. He lent money generously to the growing trade, and his beneficence was not forgotten. A year before his death in 1820, when he had been for fifty years minister of the parish, the grateful and prosperous manufacturers presented him with a silver cup engraved with lines by a local poet, one who used to refer to Scott and himself as "we poets":

> Hail, rev'rend Doctor! Dearer still
> Now when thy light is all downhill!
> There was a time, and not far gone,
> When you stood forth, and stood alone;
> When our frail bark was tempest-tost,
> And neared the shallow, rocky coast,
> You cheered the crew! A fav'ring gale
> Auspicious fills the swelling sail;
> The vessel stands again to sea,
> And rides the waves triumphantly!
> So, in the autumn of thy days,
> Accept our gratitude and praise,
> To cheer thee in thy latter end,
> Our Guide, our Pastor and our Friend.

Dr. Douglas may have thought of his friend and correspondent of so long ago and of how she would have glowed and laughed over the inscription.

It is a far cry from his day to ours but the ship still rides the waves; the mills work busily, and tweed goes far beyond its name-valley. A visit to one mill showed many bales of tweed, some in the familiar checks and plaids, but with subtle variations. Charts are first prepared to show the proportion and blending of the two colours. Taken separately the hanks of grey and black, for example, may look dull; skilfully combined they have chic. There is also the intricacy of flecked tweed, one basic colour relieved by interweaving of diverse threads. A cream warp (the wool woven lengthwise) might have a weft or cross-weave in many colours, producing many patterns; blues and greens, pinks and mauves, yellows and browns. A bale of fine and glowing stuff in a rich peacock blue lay awaiting dispatch to a famous house in Paris.

Now as a hundred years ago, much of the heavier wool comes from the Border sheep. From the fine lambswool, cashmere and mohair—still largely imported from Australia—come what one might call the glamour-tweeds, for elegant suits and dresses, even for evening gowns, the wide stoles, the soft blankets.

Once the whole process of transforming the tarry wool into thick or fine tweeds and flannels was carried out in the mill. The wool was spun here for the weaving machines. Now it is done elsewhere and arrives in hanks or "cheeses", those great round balls of wool. It is then wound on to pirns for weaving on the rollers. The colour charts show the number of threads, in each colour, to be used. These are passed through reeds, and the yarn drips down through a throstle, There is a machine for stopping broken threads, but even so, defects can linger; skilled women are employed to repair any such weakness; it is work almost as delicate as lace-making.

This particular mill employs a hundred workers, most of them women. There is plenty of work, here and in other mills and other towns, but nearly always it is for women; hence the need, stressed in every report on the Borders, for new industries. The problem of this region is not so much unemployment as depopulation, the drift away of young men.

Galashiels and Hawick are the chief mill towns. Hawick has long had a very high reputation for woollens of all kinds, hosiery, tweeds, jerseys. The skill of the workers is great, there is work enough for them—but again they are most of them women. According to one observer (Magnus Magnussen in *The Scotsman*, 24th January 1962) the men take refuge in their clubs (the Borders being addicted to clubs) in sport and in Hawick's annual festival in June, the Common Riding when the Cornet is king of the feast. It is a masculine celebration, depending on good horsemanship of which there is no lack.

Sport of every kind takes up some of the energy of the Borderers. There are the Border hunts, and there is still plenty of riding. The horse has by no means been pushed out of the scene even though Dr. Russell's gig has long since yielded to hordes of wheels. None of the Border Festivals—the Common Riding in Hawick and Selkirk, Riding the Marches in Jedburgh, the

Braw Lad's Gathering in Galashiels, would be possible without good horsemen. It is good natural riding too, not a stunt. Fishing goes on for trout and salmon, in streams and rivers; in a winter of frost there is curling; in summer there is cricket, especially in Selkirk where they play at Philiphaugh. Above all there is rugby which one commentator, Jack Dunn, has said is a Border industry rather than a mere sport or cult. They take it seriously and do it well.

These Border towns are large enough to give their inhabitants elbow room and breathing space, small enough to be distinctive, to be separate communities each with an intense local, almost a personal pride and loyalty. They are within convenient travelling distance of Edinburgh, Glasgow and the northern English towns, although the complaint, made in *The New Statistical Account*, of the lack of railroads can be made with this difference only: that the railways have come and flourished and served the community well, and that they are now in danger of being given up. This is one of the immediate and urgent problems of the Borders. The bus services have their place and value, they can take people and goods into remote villages and valleys where the railway could not be carried; but the prospect of one kind of transport only dismays most people. It would mean a bus journey into Edinburgh to join the train for London, instead of joining it at Galashiels or Hawick.

These are still country towns, even Galashiels which is perhaps the most industrial and Hawick which is so full of business. They are closely surrounded by the pastoral landscape of fields and hills, valleys and rivers and little burns. None is without its river, none but has a glimpse of the hills.

They are friendly places; everyone, or nearly everyone, knows everyone else. A housewife, coming to live in Edinburgh from Hawick found the capital a dull place, when she went shopping. In Edinburgh shops she found civility enough, but having bought or ordered her groceries, bread, dairy stuff and the rest, there was nothing to do but come home. The process had the one merit of quickness. In Hawick it was leisurely, neighbourly, couthy; in every shop, at every corner there was a pause for talk with friends and acquaintances: something about the weather, about each others' families, about last night's concert or lecture, the next meeting of the Women's Rural, the Common

Riding or other ploy. After church, on an Edinburgh Sunday, there would be polite bows and "good mornings", but when the kirk skailed in Hawick there was a fine exchange of talk.

They all have character, even personality, these towns. There is, as it were, a family likeness by which they are all known apart from the cities, from towns in Fife or Lanark or the Highlands; but each has its own look and its own ways. The visitor may find a certain similarity between Kelso and Selkirk; each on its river, each a town well planned, each with an air of France. But a little longer, and the differences will be seen, as they are seen between these towns and Melrose, Jedburgh, Galashiels. The Borderer has three loyalties—within the common British patriotism; he is a Scot, he is a Borderer, he is a townsman of his own town. There is no need to try to place the three in order of importance. Hawick takes the title of Queen of the Borders.

They could be, within their limits, the most prosperous towns in Scotland, without opulence, perhaps, but without poverty. The fact remains that the young people are leaving. Whether development is to come from within or without is still a problem.

Yet there is plenty of activity. The schools are good; Selkirk and Galashiels each has a new one. Adult Education has two centres or establishments in Galashiels. The College of Adult Education holds evening classes in a wide range of subjects, from building construction to weaving and designing, from bakery and confectionery to electrical installation, with commercial courses which include English, modern languages and Scots Law as well as typing and accountancy. The College arranges, besides, day-release classes, for which students are released from their jobs, in general school subjects like English, mathematics, physics, chemistry, and in special techniques: agricultural engineering, horticulture, agriculture, building and motor trades.

A sister institution is The Scottish Woollen Technical College with its large new buildings containing laboratories and design studios as well as lecture rooms. This is "monotechnic", that is, concentrated upon woollen manufacture in every branch of the trade. Courses, full-time and part-time, are conducted in the relevant science and technology. Students may take a B.Sc. Honours course of four years, in Textile Technology; an associateship, also of four years, in Textile Design; or a Diploma Course of three years which is equal to the pass degree at a university. A certificate is granted after two years' study, and there are other, minor courses. Fees for full-time students are £60 a year. The college is under the authority of the Scottish Education Department and under the management of an Association of nearly all the Scottish wool firms.

Life in these towns need not be dull, or absorbed by work alone. There is plenty of play, on and off the football field, cricket pitch, river and loch. Selkirk and Galashiels in especial have many clubs: musical, debating, literary, dramatic and all. There are lively debates, good lectures, concerts, plays and light opera. You may have what you fancy, you may have them all if you pay your subscription and have the energy, mental and physical.

It all rises to its zenith in May or June when every town in turn, each on its own day and in its own way, rides out to celebrate a long remembered event, to maintain old boundaries, assert old loyalties; to hold a pageant, enact a drama, keep history alive. Tourists are welcome, and the tourist influx adds to local prosperity, conditions local development; but the festivals are the towns' own affairs, conducted after an unchanging pattern and with unflagging zest.

Selkirk lives actively in the present. Selkirk has tweed-mills, one firm doing hand-weaving, and cellular blankets are produced as well as tweeds; there are dyeworks and leather-works. Some of the bakers make their own bread and the town has given its name to that delectable species of bun or tea-bread as we call it in Scotland, the Selkirk Bannock. It is a largish, round flat cake, stuffed with rasins and peel, spiced and sugared and a slice of it, with a cup of tea was all that Queen Victoria would accept, when she visited Abbotsford in 1867 and was received by Mr. Hope-Scott and his daughter and offered an elegant collation.

They keep up their archery in Selkirk and still shoot for the Silver Arrow, an old competition which lapsed for a time and was renewed in 1818 by Scott. The Royal Archers shot for it then, and were afterwards admitted as Freemen of the Burgh, and put to the test of licking the birse. The birse is a bunch of boar's bristles, once used in their trade by the souters or shoe-makers; for ceremonial purposes it was dipped in wine and drawn between the lips. A more copious and agreeable wine-drinking followed, when the company were regaled with a riddle and a

The Flodden Memorial, Selkirk

half of claret, presented by the town; a riddle is thirteen bottles
and no ill luck in that. The competition and the ceremony are
still, from time to time carried out.

About the souters, taking their name from the ancient craft
or guild of shoemakers, it was a souter, named Fletcher, who
brought the news from Flodden. To be a souter of Selkirk a
man must be born in the town. The name is not given to any
incomer, however illustrious, not even to Scott himself, the well-
loved Sheriff, whose statue in the square looks over to the
courthouse where he used to sit; not to so good a townsman
and poet as John Buchan Brown who took the name of the
town itself for his pen-name and who came there in early childhood to live all his life. The true born souters have some distinguished men among them: Mungo Park who went far into
Africa, one of the great Scottish explorers, Andrew Lang, Tom
Scott the artist who painted his own Border scenery. The most
eminent of the town's Provosts, in the past century, was that
Craig Brown who wrote the *History of Selkirkshire*, and edited,
with a memoir, the *Letters of Alison Cockburn*. He also had the
old prison, when it was given up, transformed into a library,
and presented it to the town.

The incomer will be welcomed, admitted to friendly circles
of townsfolk, to his choice of clubs; he may be elected to the
town council, even become provost; be made a freeman of the
burgh; but he will not become a souter of Selkirk. That is not
in man's power to give The souters did their best for a fellow
Borderer, Sir Alec Douglas-Home by making him a Freeman,
which was a pleasant way of ending an auld sang or of singing
that song to a cheerful new tune:

> It's up wi the Souters o' Selkirk,
> And doun wi' the Earls o' Home.

who would appear to have misconducted themselves in some
battle or foray, but we need not rake that up now.

And of course only a souter can be standard-bearer at the
Common Riding in June, remember Fletcher who bore back
the banner from Flodden and cast it in the market-place. Fletcher
is commemorated by a bronze statue, where a wreath is laid
that day of remembrance.

The day, in its unchanging ritual begins at seven o'clock when

High Street, Selkirk with Mungo Park Memorial
Hawick, Roxburghshire

the souters and other Incorporations of the Merchant Company, along with returned exiles and ex-service men gather and follow the burgh band and the pipe band down the Green to Ettrick Bank, there to meet the standard-bearer, with his cavalcade of two hundred or more good horsemen, carrying the flag he has promised to keep "unsullied and untarnished". Having forded the stream they ride, if not hell for leather, certainly at no ambling pace over the common and the marches to the top of Three Brethren Cairn, down to ford the river again and ride back into the town by the Toll and on to the market-place. Here, with all the townspeople gathered round, comes the great and moving ceremony of the Casting of the Colour. The standard-bearer waves his flag through the lovely intricate pattern of swoops and dips with which Fletcher, 450 years and more ago, announced the tragedy of Flodden. The tune "The Souters o' Selkirk" is played. The standard-bearers of the several Guilds or Incorporations, including the representative of souters over the Border and over the water who do not, in exile, forget Selkirk, follow, each with his flag. The ex-servicemen's representative casts the Union Jack while the old tune of "The Floo'ers o' the Forest" is played in remembrance of those who were wede awa' in the two great wars of this century. There is silence for a little; then cheers for the Queen and for the burgh, followed by the national anthem. After that cheerfulness does not so much creep in as storm in. The rest of that day and the following are given over to sport, games, horse-racing, fun and feasting.

And the day has been preceded by an evening which, like Christmas Eve, Hogmanay and Hallowe'en has its own ceremonies and is fit prelude to the full concert that follows. There is a procession of townsfolk to follow the burgh officer as, habited like his predecessors for centuries past, and bearing his halberd, he goes to "cry the barley"—proclaim the holiday of the Common Riding. ["Barley" is defined as a pause or truce in a children's game.] People wear ribbons or ties in the colours of the newly chosen standard-bearer. All the standards are decked with ribbons and Bussing the Flag is the rite of the standard-bearer's lass adding her ribbons to the standard. There are parties and concerts, suppers and a dance. The prudent go to bed early in order to be up in time next morning, the exuberant keep it up all night and through the small hours, finding it not worth while going to bed at all. Before the standard-bearer sets out next morning he is wished the old blessing: "Safe oot, safe in".

Hawick also has its Common Riding in June, with the Cornet and his lass leading the cavalcade. They too remember Flodden, and, more cheerfully an aftermath when Hawick lads or Callants routed a party of English who thought that the whole strength of the Borders had been drained away. They were dealt with according to their folly, and Hawick celebrates the callants' prowess. Moray McLaren who writes of it in his *Shell Guide to Scotland* calls it "spectacular to the point of hair-raising" and comments on "the almost pagan energy" with which the Riding proceeds. The spiritual heritage of the Borders goes far beyond Christianity. This is "one of the most full-blooded festivals in the country" which is saying a good deal, none of the towns being noticeably douce in their celebrations. Hawick, moreover, does not wait for the annual Common Riding to let off steam or primal energy. Here, rugby is a passion and matches between the town team, the Greens, and any rivals are far from spiritless. The song of Hawick is evocative and invocative of ancient deities: "Teribus ye Teri Odin". Who made it, who first sang it is beyond record; a full-blasted rendering must, one imagines, penetrate the halls of Valhalla and shatter the slumbrous twilight of the gods. Wagner, in fact, is not in it; he should have come to Hawick before completing "The Ring".

Kelso by comparison is peaceful: that French town which might easily be seen in Touraine with its wide square, its comely town hall, the noble five-arched Rennie bridge over Tweed, the lovely ruined abbey, the elegant Ednam House, and, on the outskirts, the splendour of Floors Castle, designed in 1818 for the first Duke of Roxburghe (a Kerr) by Sir John Vanbrugh, remodelled in 1838–49 by Playfair, further adorned in 1929 by gilded gates and new lodges. The link with France is emphasised by part of the wall round the grounds, built by French prisoners in the town, during the Napoleonic War; a long war and grim enough, but a memory of the Auld Alliance with France mellowed the relationship between French and Scots. In the grounds a holly tree marks the place where, by tradition, King James II was killed by the bursting of a cannon, at the siege of Roxburgh in 1460. As that amazing and entertaining child Marjorie Fleming put it in verse:

He was killed by a cannon splinter
Right in the middle of the winter;
Perhaps it was not at that time,
But I can find no other rhyme.

Kelso however, does not bask in dreams of the past. A busy and lively tweed town it is even now planning such modern gaieties as an ice-rink and bingo club.

Jedburgh like all the Border towns plays football with brio, and has invented the seven-a-side rugby match; but Jedburgh has its own special game of hand-ba', played at Candlemas and on Fastern E'en between the Uppies and the Downies, the upper and the lower town; played in the streets with vigour and abandon, commemorating, it is said, a gruesome game once played with the heads of English foes slain in battle or foray. In the second half of the year, in July, comes the Redeswire Ride or Riding of the Marches, which ends with the Border Games. Between those festivities Jedburgh works hard at the looms; depopulation and the drift away of men to the cities and over the Border is here, as elsewhere a problem, but there is hope of new industries. All the Border towns need easier communication by road or rail, especially the latter, with the rest of Scotland and with England.

These Ridings are old celebrations, older than the oldest buildings in the towns except the abbeys. Galashiels' Braw Lad's Gathering is recent in date, less than fifty years old, but it celebrates an event of centuries ago: a defeat of English soldiers. These had stopped by Galafoot to pluck and eat wild plums, and were there set upon by the Foresters of Galashiels and put to rout. The place, still surrounded by wild plum trees is marked by the Raid Stone. The town coat of arms has two foxes looking up at a tree with the motto "Soor Plums"; sour indeed they proved to those English.

The festival begins on a Wednesday evening in June when the Braw Lad, his Lass and their followers ride out to Torwoodlee, to be welcomed by Mr. Pringle, the laird, the Lad cuts a sod of turf and takes a stone from the old, ruined tower. Toasts are drunk, and the cavalcade rides back, the Lad bearing the sod in a satchel. Old songs are sung: "The Bonnie Woods o' Torwoodlee" and "Braw, Braw Lads". Next day comes a civic reception; on Friday the investiture of the Braw Lad and Lass with their sashes. On Saturday the real Gathering occurs: Townsfolk assemble early at the Burgh Chambers where, from the balcony, trumpeters proclaim the Midsummer Fair for which a charter was granted by James VI. The Braw Lad takes custody of the blue and white flag and rides at the head of a procession to the Raid Stone where it is placed, while he and Lads of former years kneel to have sprigs of wild plum pinned to their coats by their lasses. Then on they ride to Galafoot and over Tweed to Abbotsford, to be welcomed by Scott's great-great-great-granddaughters, given a stirrup cup and a rose for the Lad and Lass. Crossing the river again they ride to Mercat Cross where red and white roses are presented, and laid beside the thistle on the cross, to commemorate the marriage of The Thistle and The Rose, James IV with Margaret Tudor. Here too are laid the sod and the stone from Torwoodlee. From there they ride to Gala House, thence to the War Memorial, finally back to the Burgh Chambers to hand the flag back to the Provost. So ends the ritual celebration; much more follows in the way of games, sports and dancing, all the fun of the midsummer fair.

In Peebles (briefly to be noted, and only on the fringe of the Scott country), they have their Beltane Fair which ought to occur on May Day for it is the old festival of the coming of summer on the first of that month. Beltane means Baal-fire, another remembrance of ancient deities. James V, Scotland's second poet king, approved of Peebles (if the poem be correctly attributed to him):

> At Beltane when ilk bodie bownis
> At Peblis to the play,
> To hear the singin and the soundis,
> The solace suth to say
> By firth and forest furth they found,
> They graythit them full gay;
> God wait that wald they do that stound,
> For it was their Feist Day
> They said,
> Of Peblis to the play.

(*bownis*—sets out; *firth*—sheltered place or enclosure; *graythit*—dressed; *wait*—knows; *stound*—moment.)

The popular saying puts it succinctly: "Peebles for pleisure".

On Beltane Day the Cornet and his Lass ride down the High Street, and the Lass is crowned Beltane Queen. The celebrations have begun on the previous Sunday with a procession to the parish kirk. Now they take up the immemorial rite of riding the marches, out to Neidpath where they are greeted by the Warden of the Castle, over across Tweed and back. There are horse-races with the Beltane Bell as prize, concerts, dances and the Cornet's Walk. And so passes a week of pleasure tinged with tradition.

Yellow or tawny are the prevailing colours of Tweedside in autumn; the gold of the leaves grows dim, or glows like embers. Yet the autumnal tint prevails only as one colour may in a tweed subtly and richly interwoven. This web of yellow and tawny has still some green in it, bright green in the fields, dark on the hills, almost black among the firs. And the leaves, one November day, on the trees beyond the road from Peebles to Galashiels, were still golden. The road was rarely out of sight of the river, the gleam of water was part of the landscape. Brightness had by no means fallen from the air. The sun might be waning in strength but there was still warmth in the air and in the colour of the scene.

The road ran through valley and pastures with hills in the background: those hills of ballad-like names, Dunlaw, Black-law, Priesthope, Kirnie Law, on to Galashiels with its shops and mills and cheerful throng. My visit was to a printing mill where one family has, for over a hundred years produced the local paper besides much other matter. Behind a small office lies what might be called the engine room, for in its complex machinery and intense activity the printing shop recalls the heart of a ship.

To change the metaphor, *The Border Telegraph* is like Tweed, that river of many tributaries; into it have flowed other little newspapers which have had their day but by no means ceased to be, only changing their name and being merged in the greater stream. The Border towns understand diversity in unity, and their two newspapers, *The Border Telegraph* and *The Southern Reporter* act on that understanding.

The type is set up, travels to the great printing presses, then, its immediate work done, is melted down again to liquid lead. Huge rolls of paper are fed into the press to receive the imprint of news of town and county and countryside; social affairs, club meetings (Galashiels is a great place for clubs) something about the proposed and resisted plan for building between Melrose and Abbotsford.

The machine not only prints the paper but sets it in sheets, folds them and tosses them out in bundles ready to be carried out to the vans which will deliver them round the town and the neighbourhood. The work began early that morning; the people of Galashiels will have their paper to read after tea: a good tea with bread from a home bakery and slices of well-buttered Selkirk Bannock.

Some folk will settle down, after reading the paper, with a book, as their forebears did; the library still provides plenty of new literature. Others will switch on television, and many more will be off to their club. This may be the Galashiels Art Club which meets in Old Gala House, once the property of the Scotts of Gala, and which produces an occasional opera; or to the Abbotsford Scott Fellowship in the same fine house to hold a discussion or hear a lecture on Sir Walter Scott or some other Border hero.

Other townsfolk, possibly less cultured, but every man to his taste, will be discussing rugby. To quote Albert Morris (in *The Scotsman*): "Gala people . . . are apt to eat, drink and sleep rugby". The Borderers have after all, been an energetic people through the centuries, and if there are no wars or raids on at the moment, a rugby match is a fair substitute.

In spite of the masculine sport, Albert Morris finds Galashiels rather a feminine town compared with the masculine Hawick:

"A Victorian spinster, a trifle drab but not shabby, with an air of rectitude but without steely austerity, moving slowly but firmly in the frenetic rush of the modern world, with the quiet assurance of one who has a bit tucked away in the bank".

Metaphors can rarely be altogether accurate; if Galashiels is feminine she is not one of your frivolous lassies; she has plenty of commonsense, much practical ability, a good deal of interest in literature and the arts. The bit about money in the bank is sound. Money is being made in the tweed mills, in varying amounts at various levels, from owners and directors down to the lass who has gone fresh from school to learn the weaving.

Besides the tweed-making in all its stages from the hanks of wool to the lengths of cloth, thick or fine, plain or many-coloured, there is fell-mongering where sheepskins are cured, dressed and dyed to make coats and jackets and slippers. This employs male labour.

Galashiels is not merely a modern industrial town; it has its tradition culminating, as we have seen, in the Braw Lad Gathering, it has some old houses, it is a river town bordered by hills; neither is it a secluded country town. It is well placed for expansion, set on a main road, in fact at a junction of two main roads, the Edinburgh to Carlisle, and the Glasgow to Berwick and Newcastle; it is also on the main London railway line though what will happen to the railways only the powers beyond us know—if indeed they do. Edinburgh and Berwick are an hour away by train, Carlisle an hour and a half, Glasgow and Newcastle two hours.

The printing office receives orders not only from the town and district but from all over Scotland. Its own *Border Telegraph* however, concentrates on local news.

One November issue announced a plan for a regional art centre in the town, this being urged by the Galashiels Art Club. It would make enjoyment of the arts easier for a wider public, make the town more attractive to newcomers, promote tourism, perhaps by a summer Festival of the Arts. This could be linked with the proposed industrial development in new mills, factories and houses, which might become almost a new community. The Arts Club could not by itself carry so great a plan and hoped for help from local Councils.

Already there was a centre of the arts in Old Gala House, the neighbouring Public Library and their precincts. These might be enlarged to include a small theatre with a restaurant, a picture gallery, a Border museum. Already in its twenty years of life, the Arts Club had done a great deal for the culture of the town and the Borders generally; Old Gala House had been bought and furnished, concerts, plays, operas had been produced, there had been exhibitions of paintings and of photography. The membership with that of affiliated clubs, some twenty-eight of them added up to two thousand people.

The *Telegraph* reported a dog show held in Melrose, by the Selkirk and District Canine Society, with entrants ranging from spaniels, hounds and pointers to miniature dachshunds, "any

variety of toy", and a satisfactory number of Cairns, West Highland terriers and Border terriers. Of dogs on the Borders more
will be told.

Sports news was prominent: "Gala Win Easily" headed the
rugby page. "The Braw Lads were on top in all phases of the
game, but in the first half they were unable to turn their superi-
ority into points". Selkirk, too, had been victorious at Philhaugh
in a comparatively peaceful battle: "After a series of heavy
defeats this success must give the Souters encouragement for
the future".

In soccer the local team, Gala Fairydean, had won against
Vale of Leithen. Cricket clubs were meeting to appoint captain
and committee, and a weekly coaching of young players had
begun at the College for Further Education.

The hottest of hot news was the Border Development Scheme,
and that must have a chapter to itself. In that autumn and early
winter of 1966 the Blue Bonnets were waving furiously, as they
still are from time to time. There were other controversies
besides, and other threats to the present way of life.

One lay in the suggested closure of the railway between Galashiels and Edinburgh to the north, Galashiels and Carlisle to
the south. The attitude of the would-be destroyers resembled
that ascribed to Marie Antoinette who, on hearing that the poor
had no bread is said to have replied: "Let them eat cake".

The proposed alternative to rail travel is always to use more
private cars. The fact that quite a number of people even in our
affluent society cannot afford a car, or are incapable of driving
one or simply do not want one, has not occurred to those aboli-
tionists. The other alternative of bus travel results in more
crowding on roads already over-crowded, too much heavy
transport, slower journeys, inconvenience in stowing away lug-
gage, less frequent services, less convenient stations than on the
railway.

Yet another revolt was raging against the Private Member's
Bill, proposed by the local Member of Parliament, David Steel,
to legalise Abortion under a number of circumstances, medical,
physical, mental and social. The opposition has come not only
from Catholics but from citizens of every religious denomination, and from doctors and nurses. Few Bills have been more
passionately discussed.

A newspaper must deal with world affairs, a provincial paper with those of its own region; but it need not be earth-bound. *The Border Telegraph* deals with astronomy. In this particular issue it had a survey of The November Sky: Venus out of sight, Mars and Jupiter appearing as morning stars "only of interest to early risers", Saturn brilliant, Orion dominant, Sirius appearing from the southern hemisphere.

"Her evening appearance is always fascinating, but it will be almost the midnight hour before this bright star can be seen. Sirius outshines any of the fixed northern hemisphere stars in her brilliance. . . . Sometimes her brilliance will even penetrate a filmy cloud." She can now be found "casting a seeming searching eye on her brothers and sisters in the northern hemisphere for a few hours only, before she sinks again in the south-west."

Capella is rising, Vega "the star of the summer nights" is sinking with little chance of showing her full beauty. It is only briefly, as she descends, these winter evenings, that her "characteristic glory" is realised; but she still adds "a distinctive sparkle to the increasing darkness of the coming winter mornings".

The Pleiades have risen, Castor and Pollux the Heavenly Twins have appeared. The glory and pageantry of the sky rise above the Border hills, and above the gleam of Tweed and Gala Water.

VIII

SHEEP COUNTRY

What meaneth then this bleating of sheep in mine ears?

—1 Samuel XV:14

In green pastures.

—Psalm 23

The folds shall be full of sheep.

—Psalm 65

THE sheep country has not changed much, and the shepherd on the hills works very much in the way of his father and grandfather; down in the valley the agricultural farms have known great developments, more progress through machinery.

The flocks make the calendar. The rams go out in the autumn, lambing begins in spring. It may be as early as January, as late as April. The fleece-clipping is done in June and July. Lamb sales are held in August, that of rams in October. Some of the ewe lambs are kept to be reared as hoggs (young sheep before they have lost their first fleece); at a year old or a year and a half, when they are called gimmers, they enter the breeding stock, and breed for five years. They are then sold as cast ewes.

Border Cheviot and Linton Blackface are the chief breeds. Farms are from 1,000 to 3,000 acres, and one shepherd may look after anything from twenty to thirty score of sheep. The Blackface graze mostly on the hirsels or heathery pastures, the Cheviots on grass. From a hundred ewes eighty-five or so lambs are expected; that is, in the hill flocks; those in the valley have more lambs to the flock, sometimes 115 from a hundred ewes. Here the breed is sometimes crossed with Border Leicesters. Lambing comes earlier than in the hill pastures. And the valleys and lowland farms are often mixed: pastoral, dairy, arable.

The monks began the wool-trade and the cultivation of land.

They left no direct inheritors. It was not until the eighteenth century that agriculture began to develop in Scotland generally, and notably on the Borders. In 1727 The Society for Improving the Knowledge of Agriculture, recently founded, included two Border lairds, Lord Lothian (a Kerr) and Lord Elibank (a Murray). It was a Roxburghshire farmer, Dawson of Herperton, who first grew turnips in the open field.

One of the worthies of the Court of Session, Henry Home, Lord Kames, his judicial title taken from his birthplace in Berwickshire, who is mentioned by Scott in the first chapter of *Redgauntlet*, published in 1776 a remarkable treatise: "The Gentleman Farmer. Being an Attempt to Improve Agriculture by Subjecting it to the Test of Rational Principles". He was a practical farmer himself during the long vacation from the Law Courts. His book was dedicated to another Borderer, Sir John Pringle, President of The Royal Society.

Kames writes about the clearing, ploughing and preparation of land for sowing; about planting for food such various crops as wheat, rye, barley, oats, beans, potatoes and turnips. These last two were by this time commonly grown in field.

"It animates me to have opportunity of giving directions about a crop, that the best farmers in this country have now taken into their plan of husbandry, and that does not escape even small farmers. Nor am I acquainted with a single instance in Scotland where the turnip fairly begun have been relinquished. . . . No person ever deserved better of a country than he who first cultivated turnip in the field."

Kames begins his chapters on the growing of crops with a description of "the capital object of a farm, that of raising plants for the nourishment of man and other animals". Dealing with the others, he advises the use of oxen rather than farm-horses. They are patient and tractable, cheaper to feed, content with grass in summer, hay and oat-straw in winter, healthier, needing little care. Horses are prone to disease and accidents. If an ox were lamed and thus disabled for work he could be fattened and sold for meat. Lord Kames waxes irate over the ignorance and stupidity of Scots farmers in ignoring this patient and helpful beast.

In general, however, he finds much to approve: "Some years ago, farmers in Scotland were ignorant and indolent; nothing was to be seen but weeds and trash, not a single field in order. People habituated to such objects never once thought of doing better. Skill in agriculture is spreading gradually in Scotland; and young people acquire some knowledge by sight, even before they think of practice."

The lairds and landowners had been as much to blame as the farmers; it was for them to show how to put care and money into the land, and thus reap profit.

The eighteenth century, that golden age in Scottish literature and learning and in social life, was, if not a golden age in agriculture, at least the beginning of progress towards wealth on the land, and the Borders were well forward.

It was, however, then as now, sheep more than crops, or cattle. Dr. Alexander ('Jupiter') Carlyle, the minister of Inveresk tells of the progress of the young Duke and Duchess of Buccleugh through their estates, from Hawick to Langholm, in 1762. All along the road the shepherds formed a guard of honour with their sheep, displaying the true wealth of the countryside.

J. B. Selkirk's old countryman recalled his youth, at the beginning of the nineteenth century when there was "no wheels but on a barrow". There were carts enough a hundred years later, but the swiftest change has probably come in less than fifty years. The modern farm would seem to him to be in a new world altogether; that of the 1920s would have been still recognisable.

In *The Third Statistical Account of Selkirkshire* the owner Mr. William Pate, of one large farm, mixed pastoral, dairy and arable describes the changes over forty years. He has about fifty young cattle; heifers are reared for stock, bull calves are sold, Friesians are kept for a dairy herd. The sheep are mostly North Country Cheviots, four hundred of them, and about sixty Linton Blackface on the hill pasture, all under the care of one shepherd, with help from the farmer's sons. These ewes produce 750 lambs a year and thirty-two hundredweight of wool. No lambs are kept after October, the pasture being needed for the ewes. In winter they are fed on hay and turnips supplemented by special feeding stuff. Every year some Cheviot lambs are bought for stock.

The hundred and fifty acres under plough produce oats, barley, turnips and potatoes; and it is on this part of the farm that the change is so great.

The horse has almost gone, not, as Lord Kames advised, to make way for the ox, but to be replaced by machinery. The tractor is everywhere in use. Forty years ago two men, each with a single-furrow plough and two horses took sixteen days to plough twenty-two acres, and this was good going, almost a record. In 1964 two men with three-furrow tractor ploughs took only three days. The essential work of ploughing sowing reaping goes on but the pace and rhythm have been altered. So it is with hay-making; the hay once cut, coiled and ricked is now picked up in one process by a mechanical baler.

The Pastoral Society (founded by Lord Napier) continues, along with the modern National Farmers' Union and the Young Farmers' Club. The Edinburgh and East of Scotland College of Agriculture, founded in 1901, sends lecturers, and experts to give advice on developments. This is to farming what the Galashiels Technical College is to the woollen industry.

The Forestry Commission has planted many trees, at Traquair and Elibank and in Yair Hill Forest: oak, ash, birch and conifers. But afforestation is limited by the high value of grazing land. The sheep come first; wool is wealth and work and growth, although afforestation also means more work for men, one man for every hundred acres.

Changes have come with machinery and other inventions, but the ways of nature do not change. This hill country retains both its beauty and its danger. One enemy is still unconquered—the snow.

The past winter of 1966–67 has been tolerable, even pleasant for days at a time (of the behaviour of the early spring more will be said later). It was, for the most part, an open winter as we say in Scotland; not locked by frost and snow. It can happen like this, it can happen far otherwise. Nature rules these hills and valleys, men and beasts are subservient, and if they are wise, respectful. Her power is felt. The long winter of 1962–63 is not forgotten.

It began with snow in November which aroused forebodings, but the full bitterness was not felt until the New Year. All through January and most of February 1963 the whole of Britain, from Caithness and Sutherland down to Devon and Somerset was beleaguered by winter. On the Borders drifts piled up on roads and railway, bringing the agelong menace of isolation, hunger, even of death. There is now a mechanism of relief and rescue unknown even fifty years ago, but no mechanism can altogether overcome the soft, implacable force of piling, drifting, recurring snow.

The New Year dawned in storm. On 2nd January roads were blocked: the road over Soutra, that between Carter Bar and Jedburgh, Carter Bar and Hawick. Drifts nine or ten feet high piled up, farms and cottages were cut off. On the foothills of the Cheviots, sheep were buried in snow. Shepherds were working round the clock to dig out their flocks and restore them to life. One man had to dig out twenty-eight.

Human life was in danger too from isolation. Men from the Automobile Association with Council workers and others from the farms dug for hours to reach a farm near Jedburgh where a woman must be taken to hospital to have her baby. They dug through ten feet drifts for three miles; about half a mile from the farm they were met by local men who had managed to bring a tractor. And so to hospital and a safe delivery and all well with mother and child.

Helicopters dropped food and fodder for men and sheep and cattle. The problem of winter feeding began to be troublesome. Hay would become scarce and dear. Mail vans and other deliveries were, to put it mildly, hampered; post-men had to wade through drifts, across fields, a farmer in Lauder walked to the main road to collect deliveries.

A shepherd and his wife were cut off in their cottage on the Lammermuirs for sixteen days. The valiant and merciful service of helicopters continued; food came down like manna. They could drop food but they could not always land. Many families in the hill cottages were cut off; at Blackcleugh near Hawick a woman was ill. The helicopter came and hovered but could not land, either to take her to hospital or to bring a doctor to her.

Railway blockages were so bad that at one point the heavy over-hang of snow had to be blasted away with dynamite. More and more roads were blocked, that over Carter Bar being the worst snow trap.

The rain came but not with deliverance. The brief thaw was followed by more frost, this second stage worse than the first. "Hell on ice" was one description of the roads. The whole south-east corner of Scotland was beseiged by winter, and to add to the misery and menace came fog. Again came a mock thaw, worse than a continuance of the frost, for it left wet slush on top of hard snow, and then it froze again.

It was a long siege by General Winter and all his forces, subtle and implacable. Snow continued, off and on, without any real relaxation from Christmas 1962 till late February 1963. Yet life —and fun—went on, even as they do in war-time. The Border spirit is respectful to the forces of nature but it does not give way; Borderers have their faults but lassitude is not among them. Parties and pleasures continued. In Selkirk the British Legion gave one for children, the Red Cross entertained the old folk. Local dances and other merriments enlivened the long spell of cold. And in Melrose, in Christmas week, the Freemasons held their ritual celebration of the Eve of St. John the Evangelist. In a torchlight procession, with the wind blowing hail and snow against them, they walked from the Market Place, led by a pipe band, to the abbey, with one of the Brothers in front, carrying a sword. Their torches had lit the dark Market Place and now they lit the abbey as the procession circled the nave, throwing the light high on the old walls. The sang "The Flowers o' the Forest".

And at last it ended, that bitter winter and spring came again, and the lambs were born, the fields and hills were green again, though it was long before the hills were clear of snow. On a bright spring day on Tweedside or in Ettrick or Yarrow it is easy to forget the darkness. This is country as old as the hills, yet recurringly youthful, as a town can never be young; for youthfulness means new life, and this comes to the Borders with new-born lambs and calves; with bird-song and with bleating and the rush of water as the full burns and rivers flow; with subtle and varied green on the trees and the grass bright emerald; the spring flowers in bloom, snowdrops and crocus giving place to daffodils, narcissi, and scylla: white and gold and blue splashing the woods and gardens.

Winter has its amusements, both outdoor and indoor. Every number of the Border newspapers has full reports of rugby and soccer matches, played and reported with equal zest. Wedding parties, dances, concerts, club dinners and suppers recur here as elsewhere; one society is peculiar to this sheep country, and that is the Yarrow and Ettrick Pastoral Society which has

Ettrick Water near Ettrick, Selkirkshire
Tweed Valley, looking west towards Elibank

reached its diamond jubilee, a respectable age, and is in descent from the earlier society founded in 1819. The dinner in celebration was held in November instead of in January, the latter month being so crowded with Burns Suppers. A columnist in *The Southern Reporter*, Edwin Hector, described the evening, which began for him with a drive through moonlit Yarrow valley to the hotel. No artificial celebration this; the Pastoral Society is part of the pattern of Ettrick Forest, of this sheep country, of the ancient craft of sheep breeding with its traditional skill and wisdom. The company came from Selkirk and from all the country round, from hill and valley farms. "A grand night in Yarrow"—it could be the title of a poem in the manner of J. B. Selkirk, it was the heading of an excellent bit of prose, well flavoured with Scots. You do not have to, indeed you must not put Scots words and idioms within quotation marks if you are writing for a Border paper.

"Where else than Yarrow can you talk with the first man to motor livestock to St. Boswells?"—This was James Amos who could recall that transport. The guest of honour—Michael Noble —speaking in praise of the craft of sheep breeding said that the modern shepherd must be something of a chemist as well; one might add he has to be something of a doctor.

Edwin Hector writes with lively memories: of another long winter on the Borders, in 1925, when he was met at the station by a horse-drawn sledge and driven home over hard-packed snow, through the silent, sparkling night; something of an enchanted journey for him, "but the horse was glad to be home". Writing of a Christmas tea given for the old folk, last December, he tells of the old lady he met whose father had kept a drysalter's shop, and remembered customers coming in to buy "a wee sarkie for my lampie"; otherwise, a new mantle for the gas lamp. The Borders may not be quite so given to diminutives as Aberdeen and that airt, but they still diminish words affectionately.

For Selkirk the last event of the year was the Meet of the Duke of Buccleuch's Hunt in the Market Square on New Year's Eve, Hogmanay, which last year fell on a Saturday. The year thus ended as it had begun, for the Hunt had met on New Year's Day 1966; welcomed by the Provost, a stirrup cup duly offered—a good run following by the Haining, Riddell and Greenhill, ending in two kills. It was, the account says, as good

Lone St. Mary's Loch

as a Common Riding—and what better praise can be given by
a souter of Selkirk?

The souters are determined to keep the Common Riding to
themselves, a local rite, a local memorial. In the spring of 1967
Edinburgh invited the souters to produce their Riding in the
capital, as part of a pageant or parade in Princes Street. This was
refused, and even without Border blood one must sympathise.
All pageant and ceremonial must, if it is to be true and living,
be rooted in the land where it is performed. Edinburgh has her
full share of history easy to be represented in action and movement; but a souter did not ride back there with his flag, to bring
the news from Flodden Field which lay so near Selkirk. If Fletcher
rode again, a guardian ghost, some midnight in June he might
not recognise the town, and he would find it decidedly more
alive and cheerful—in fact hilarious—than on that day of dolour
when he brought the flag. But the Border speech would still
greet him; and once over the river he would be on familiar
ground. He would know the purpose of this riding.

History, an ancient craft, a pattern of landscape—all these are
interwoven in the beauty of this sheep country—Upper or Lower
Tweeddale, Ettrick or Yarrow or Teviot, down to the verge of
Northumberland or up in Peeblesshire close to the west country.
The townsfolk from the past, whether of Selkirk or Hawick,
Kelso, Melrose or Jedburgh might if they made a brief return
from where, at the gates of Paradise the birk grows fair enough,
be at first bewildered. But a shepherd of another day would
know his pastures, hail his successor as fellow, commend or
criticise his way with the sheep but not find them new.

The hills and the valley pastures, the rivers and waters and
burns would still receive him as they would a meditative wanderer.

"To walk across the heather on a breezy August day . . . to
hear the whir of the grouse as they sail over the sea of colour,
or the snort of the black-faced sheep . . . to trace the winding
burn through the deep cut it has hollowed out for itself through
the ages . . . to watch it drop over the rock, overhung with
rowan and hazel and fern, into the deep pool below round which
it whirls and whirls . . . to follow its course and hear it singing
as it goes, even though the active little dipper keeps it company . . . to note the lonely herd's house at the forkins with the

blue peat reek curling lazily above the old ash trees at the gable
—to experience all these is to go up at least into the third heaven."

That was not written a century or so ago, by a man of letters
and leisure. It is quoted in *The Southern Reporter* as the account
of a Border farmer of today. And only yesterday, as time goes
in these parts (to be precise about seventy years ago) that good
Borderer by blood and by affection if not by birth-place, John
Buchan, caught the spell of this hill country, knew the good
companionship of its men.

Buchan was born in Perth (in 1875) the son of a Free Kirk
minister; his father went to another charge in Fife, where other
children were born, Anna, William and Walter. But all their
holidays were spent in Tweeddale, at Broughton in Peeblesshire,
on the borders of the Scott country, within reach of places
Scott knew; in the hill country, the country of waters and
burns, the sheep country. Mrs. Buchan's family, the Mastertons,
had been sheep-farmers for generations. For her children, the
old farm was home whence they returned reluctantly to Fife. "The
Borders were to us a holy land which it would have been sacri-
lege to try to join on to our common life"—so Buchan has written
in *Memory-Hold-the-Door*. Their play was in a glen where a
burn joined a larger water which in turn flowed into Tweed.
Like J. B. Selkirk, like Andrew Lang in boyhood and like
Randal and Jean in his story, these late Victorian bairns knew the
incomparable delight of a burn that had run with many a turn,
and had a trout pool with a beech tree in the background. There
was a hollow in the hill nearby, too, which might very well
have been Arthur's sleeping place. It was a perfect background
for acting games which came very near reality, which were
true drama.

John grown older went further afield, fishing up the waters,
climbing the hills, making friends with the shepherds: "men of
the long stride and clear eye... a great race. I have never known
a greater". They were sober and diligent, God-fearing men,
masters of their craft, "grave livers" Wordsworth had called
them; but the fighting blood was in them—and a drop of the
poacher's or the reivers. They were sure of themselves and
with security came a natural dignity they were born aristocrats.
Buchan who continued in literature the tradition of his beloved
Sir Walter Scott, had his hero's love of ordinary people, of

country folk; he knew and spoke the soft Border Scots. Best of all he liked those shepherds, their wisdom, their independence, their tolerance; their ancestors in the early days of Christianity in Scotland may have stoned Merlin to death as a wizard, but a certain mellowness has come since then, and the fanatic zeal of the south-west has halted at the borders of Tweeddale.

The young Buchan found himself admitted into their company: "into the secrets of a whole lost world of pastoral". That world was by no means lost in his boyhood; drovers still went past the farm at Broughton, taking their cattle to Falkirk Tryst, or from the Highlands down to England.

His first novel was set in this region: *John Burnet of Barns*. His first book of essays, *Scholar Gipsies* published when he was twenty-one, is a book of the Borders. One of his ploys was to fish by night in a water among the hills. It was August, and after a day of sun the sky was brilliant, the hills stood dark and strong against its luminance, the flies glittered like fire-flies, the trout had a thousand colours. He had a good catch; and then he was hailed by the shepherd of Redeswirehead, striding along in his plaid, a horn-handled stick in one hand, a gun in the other. He was out for an old vixen fox that had many a slaughter to her discredit. They talked a little, they spent the night on the heather; the sunset faded, stillness and darkness came; the boy slept, and was awakened by a shot. The shepherd of Redeswirehead had shot the fox; her depredations were ended, vengeance was done. This man had no book-learning but no scholar could know his books better than he knew bird-life and the country and the sky; he could tell the time within a quarter of an hour by the sky, and "could walk by night in a snowstorm to any place in Tweeddale"—which many another, though skilled and country-wise could not do.

The shepherds were well-living, God-fearing men; others less reputable were no less good companions: the vagrant Sandy Scott, among them, with whom Buchan tramped a long day's walk through upper Tweeddale, over the burn of Kingledores, to Talla Vale and Tweedsmuir, by many little streams—Menzion, Fuid and Cor, to a water where Sandy cut a long willow rod, thick at the base, thin and pliable at the top, tied on a line, gut (he wore some on his shabby bonnet) and hook, cast most dexterously and landed a pounder, followed by other four. This was in June, a day of light and of stillness broken by country sounds: the murmur of bees, the twittering of sandpipers, the far-off bleating of sheep. The moorland stretched far beyond them to the distant hills, country known only to the shepherds and to vagrants. That night the vagrant and the boy slept out, in a shed half full of bracken; broiled some of the trout for breakfast, left some as rent for their lodging.

Buchan writes of two gentlemen of leisure known in his boyhood: "One belonged to a most respectable class; the other was the essence of disrespectability". The former was a country clergyman, a scholar and a gentleman, a man of devout life and learning whose hobby was fishing in Tweed "where he said he found more inspiration than in St. Augustine". The other was a tramp, shabby, bold and cheerful, who lived as he liked, fishing a good deal, poaching a little, working at times, helping with the lambs; a skilled angler, with long hazel wand for rod, and deep pockets for fishing basket; a natural aristocrat, with leisure and independence, a keen sense of enjoyment, as much security as he wanted, a full-bodied personality. Such vagrants were in true descent from Edie Ochiltree. The Scott country and its people, as Scott himself knew it, was still known to young John Buchan. He was the more alert to its character for coming to it from the very borders of the Borders on the western side. Broughton lies close to Lanarkshire; upper Tweed is very near Clydesdale and Annandale, but there is a difference wider than can be measured in miles. In Tweeddale there is "an epitome of landscape . . . a country of surprises . . . of contradiction, blended into harmony by that subtle Border charm". The people had the same quality of contrast and surprise, being at once stern and gentle, prudent and reckless, serious and humorous. In this boyhood, a hundred years after Scott's own, there was still much oral tradition of old tales; not only those of the Borders but those of epic and classical legends. The people were not, on the whole, fanatical in religion, having more than a touch of worldliness in their piety; but they were hot and zealous in politics. In this, most of all, lingered the spirit of the ancient feuds.

There is the story of an old shepherd, dying at peace with his Maker, hoping for no better Paradise than "Bourhope at a reasonable rental". The same mind was in Fisher Jamie in one of Buchan's own poems, who, for his virtue and valour had merited Heaven but would care little for heavenly music; the tunes he loved were the song of Tweed in spate or of Talla "loupin' owre its linns"; the joy he had known was fishing, and not always strictly lawful. But the Apostles were kindly men and had once been fishers themselves, so Jamie might well be lent a rod and line, hook and bait, and slipping out by the back door of his heavenly mansion, hasten to some waterside:

> And syne, wi' saumon on his back,
> Catch't clean against the Heavenly law,
> Wi' Heavenly byliffs on his track
> Gaun linkin' doun some Heavenly shaw.

Professor Veitch compared the Borders with Greece, for aspect and for its breed of scholars and poets; and perhaps there is a further affinity, in this earthiness, this mingling of the homely with the heavenly which makes no bad kind of religion.

Buchan admitted himself a nympholept; one enamoured of running water. This is "the key of the landscape" in the Borders; in whichever county one travels—in Scott's own Selkirk and Roxburgh, in Peebles and in Berwick, the waters set the pattern, whether they be little burns running with many a turn, or great rivers running wide and deep: Tweed or Teviot, Ettrick or Yarrow, or the little waters of countless names. And these last are, according to Buchan, of two types, the highland and the lowland. The former fall in pools among the rocks, with birch, ash and alder growing near; the latter have slight falls, not steep or tumultuous, and a long run between pools. They are the more common; but the highland type is found at Merlin's grave, Powsail Burn. He found a difference too in the fish. Salmon are "those brazen creatures" from the outer seas, but trout are "humble and pious", aware of the hush, the almost mystic peace of sunset and dusk. For all their piety, he would gladly catch them—as Andrew Lang had done, as Fisher Jamie did.

John Buchan, like Scott, personifies the vigorous diversity of talent found in men of the Border. Though not bred to the law he was to prove himself a man of affairs, an administrator, a vice-regal governor. In his chosen career of letters he was to be a novelist in the Scott tradition, a biographer, an historian, an essayist. His most popular tales were set far from Tweed, though Border names recur, and sometimes a visit to the Borders. For many readers his best book is his *Life of Scott*. Yet all his brave and thrilling stories of adventure are in descent from the Border ballads, as were Scott's poems and novels, and sometimes there is a glimpse of the uncanny and the magic which dwells in the Border hills.

For Buchan's sister Anna—O. Douglas by her pen-name— the Border country was also dear; and her most delightful novels are set in Peebles and its county which they portray with affection tinged with gentle mockery. There is nothing in them of magic or terror, danger or excitement; yet in one of the most placid; *Pink Sugar* there is a scrap of dialogue which holds a note of the old ferocity. The heroine is visiting a shepherd and his wife. Their daughter comes home from shopping in the village, more tardily than her mother approves, and is accused of lingering in the shop to gossip. "I could rin a sword through ye," says her mother which the daughter hears with unbroken calm. The son is reporting to his father about the sheep sales and about an extortionate price demanded by one man. Asked his reply, Willie says he told the man he could take his sheep to hell. His father approves; but a moment later, when Willie cannot answer another question, his sire comments bitterly: "Willie kens nocht ava. I'm rale vexed for him" as for one mentally defective.

Truly it is a country and a people of contrasts and surprises.

IX

DOGS OF THE BORDERS

The stag-hounds weary of the chase
Lay stretched upon the rushy floor,
And urged in dreams the forest race
From Teviot-stone to Eskdale moor.
—Scott, *Lay of the Last Minstrel*

MEN, sheep and dogs make a natural trinity on the Borders. Horses are part of its history, some famous, some nameless: the horses that carried men into battle and home again, with tidings of victory or dolour; the horses ridden by the reivers; by lovers escaping from pursuing parents and brothers; and, of course the fairy steeds of the Queen of Elfhame with True Thomas behind her, and of her host, with Tamlane praying to be rescued by his love Janet.

They are still part of Border life: at the Riding of the Marches in the Border towns, in the Hunt, in farm work and on some roads. But even more of a friend and helper to a man is his dog; here in this sheep country it is the closest alliance possible, for the dog is not only a comrade but a working partner.

The greatest of Borderers was the greatest of dog-lovers.

A book has been written (by E. Thornton Cook) about Sir Walter's dogs; a large anthology could be gathered of all his references to them, all his descriptions in the poems and novels; dogs real and imagined, the latter deriving from the former. There must have been a dog on guard, as well as the shepherd, when the little lame boy lay in his sheepskin beside his grandfather's sheep at pasture. Dogs went with him on his rides, dogs sat by him in his study. Lockhart has described the study in Castle Street, open to invasion by the children and by Maida the noble hound who went with them to Abbotsford, died there, full of years and honour, and was buried at the door, under a rough effigy of himself, used as a mounting-block. "Sleep soundly, Maida, at your master's door" is his epitaph, thus Englished from the Latin.

There was Camp, too, who had been "got by a black and tan English terrier called Doctor, out of a thoroughbred brindled bull bitch"; an excellent mixture: a dog of infinite loyalty, intelligence and sagacity, and, according to his master, of considerable "gaiety and drollery". When he was too old to follow Scott on his rides, he stayed quietly at home, ready for the bidding: "The Sheriff's coming home by the ford", or "The Laird's coming by the hill", when he would make for the proper meeting-place. When he died, Scott refused a dinner invitation, because of the death of an old friend; Camp was buried in the garden in Castle Street within sight of his master's writing-table. He appears in the portrait by James Saxon and in that by Raeburn.

We have seen the arrival at Abbotsford from Ashestiel of the new laird and lady, with their children, maids and dogs both old and young, and all the other animals. From that day onward Abbotsford never lacked dogs. As was only fitting for a Borderer, Scott acquired Border terriers; "cruet dogs", he called them: Spice the most famous, Pepper and Mustard, Ginger and all.

When financial ruin fell heavily upon him he thought of his dogs: "It is foolish, but the thought of parting from these dumb animals has moved me more than any of the painful reflections I have put down", he wrote in his Journal. "Poor things, I must get them kind masters".

He did not, after all, have to live bereft. Dogs were with him to the end. He commended them to Lockhart's care when he went abroad on that last, vain quest for health; they welcomed him home and gave him comfort.

This love of dogs was shared by his family. Lady Scott had a cherished little terrier, Ourisk, devoted to her, reserved, even unfriendly towards others; but when she died, Ourisk came to Anne, lay on her bed, and adopted this new mistress. It gave Anne a poignant thrust of both comfort and grief.

The grandchildren too loved dogs. Johnny Lockhart played with them when he was well enough, and they followed him when he rode, on pony or in chair, round the grounds. Charlotte as a small lady of two, delighted her grandfather by quelling a riot. Sophia wrote to Lockhart how "Baby" strode in among the quarrelling dogs with a stick in her hand and a look in her eye. The Lockharts too had their dogs, in London.

Some years later, when Sophia was dead, and Charlotte was from home, with her governess, Lockhart wrote her a most endearing and entrancing letter: written as if by her Border terrier Ginger, duly signed with that name and with a neatly drawn bone, giving all the domestic news.

The "cruet dogs" were of good Border breed. They are made immortal in *Guy Mannering*. When young Brown who is really the heir to Ellangowan comes to Scotland he is accompanied by his faithful Wasp; at the inn where he encounters Dandie Dinmont, the latter looks benevolently on the little dog:

"A bonny terrier, sir, and a fell chield at the vermin, I warrant him—that is, if he's been weel entered, for it a' lies in that".

Thus begins a good friendship. Dandie stresses the value of training: "Beast or body, education should aye be minded".

He tells of his own six terriers; "Auld Pepper and Auld Mustard, young Pepper and young Mustard, little Pepper and little Mustard" all of them entered, trained, and put to the hunt against stoats and weasels, rats, tods (or foxes) and brocks (or badgers). The Duke himself—of Buccleuch—has sent for one of his Peppers and Mustards. "Siccan a day as we had wi' the foumarts (polecats) and the tods, and siccan a blythe gae-down as we had against e'en".

When, after their adventure and escape on the way, Dandie and Brown arrive at the farm of Charlieshope they are welcomed exuberantly by all the Peppers and Mustards besides other breeds unnamed; Wasp is accepted. The next few days are given to sport, to a fox hunt not conducted by orthodox rules but necessary and effective, and to Scott's own favourite salmon-spearing. All the dogs, the terriers "sent forward under the care of a shepherd" while "mongrel, whelp and cur of low degree filled up the burden of the chorus" hunt the tod to his death.

Scott adds a note in characteristic manner:

"The race of Pepper and Mustard are in the highest estimation at this day, not only for vermin-killing but for intelligence and fidelity. Those who, like the Author, possess a brace of them, consider them as very desirable companions".

Dandie Dinmont whose name is perpetuated in the breed spoke for all the dogs of the Borders when he said: "Education should aye be minded". There is no place in rural life for pets and lap dogs. A dog, hound or terrier, collie or mongrel must be trained, must have his place and his job. He is all the more loved for not being spoiled; he is accorded the dignity due to his nature and function.

This is true above all of the sheep dog who more than any other is friend and partner. There is no closer relationship anywhere between man and beast, none in which the four-footed comrade is treated with more serious respect. The horse is a helper, once necessary still often needed; any decent dog is on terms of mutual respect, affection and dependence, with his owner; but the sheep dog shares with the shepherd the care and management of the flock. He helps to guide and protect them. The shepherd cannot do all the work alone; the dog is, in a sense, an interpreter. He understands human speech and gesture, he knows the nature of the sheep more intimately than a human mind can, even the most sympathetic. He translates the master's bidding into action understood by the sheep.

Scott's picture of winter in the Introduction to the First Canto of *Marmion* includes a sheep dog:

> The shepherd shifts his mantle's fold,
> And wraps him closely from the cold;
> His dogs no merry circles wheel,
> But shivering follow at his heel.

Merry circling is permitted, for a dog must release his high spirits; but the phrase "follow at his heel" is the secret of training. The intricate lesson must be learned of when to come to heel and follow, when to go forth and round in and bring back the sheep. For a domestic dog the bidding "to heel" may be enough; the sheep dog must be further directed, trained to the last degree of judgement, self-reliance and co-operation. He must be of one mind with his master, knowing exactly what is asked of him; close enough in animal sense and instinct to understand their need for guidance and protection, close enough to the shepherd to interpret his bidding to the flock.

Sheep, according to James Hogg, the Ettrick Shepherd, have little character "save that of natural affection" which is strong in them. Otherwise, it is "a stupid, indifferent animal, having few wants and fewer expedients".

This is a realistic but not unkind judgement. Hogg noted the profound love of a ewe for her lamb, her grief if she lost one, her need for another to feed and cherish; he noted also the attachment of sheep to one place.

Sheep, in fact, need guidance; docile and meek, they are easily disturbed. A good dog knows this and spares them all the disturbance he can. Hogg calls him "the most docile and affectionate of the whole animal creation" and to these amiable qualities he adds intelligence and resourcefulness.

The Ettrick Shepherd has a tale of his own uncle, John Hoy, who, after attending the yearly Sacrament one Sabbath morning, wished also to hear the afternoon sermon; but he must have the ewes gathered in by a certain hour. A hint to his dog was enough; off she went to the hills and brought the flock safely in.

This man's dogs were all famous for their skill in "*hirsel-running*; that is, gathering sheep at a distance". Hogg points out that sheep-dogs vary more than any other in their variety of talent and characteristics; and these varieties are transmitted from one generation to another as in a human family. Some are skilled at gathering in the sheep from the hills "but can never be taught to command sheep close around", others may fail on the hillside but be adept at managing the flock round the bught or fold. "Some again excel in a kind of social intercourse", understanding all that is said not only directly to themselves but about them and about the sheep.

John Hoy had a bitch called Tub whom young Hogg once saw gathering in the sheep from the hill at the head of a glen, while her master stood, out of sight, on another hill; all the dog could hear was the echo of his voice or whistle.

Another, called Nimble, rescued a hundred ewes in the snow "one drifty day" (a vivid word). The shepherd looked long and vainly for them, fearing them lost in the drifting snow; at last he sent out Nimble who, following their scent found them and stood guard; without a further bidding she would not bring them in. Her master gave "the gathering word" and with the utmost swiftness she gathered and brought them home.

Hogg himself had good dogs with whom he shared his food, and a corner of his plaid when the rain came. "The consequence was that I generally had the best dogs in all the country". Best of them all was Sirrah, though not for any social intercourse, being, at first, sullen and surly. This was not without cause. Hogg had bought him, for a guinea, a lean, starved cur, from a drover who had used him ill. And Sirrah had the basic virtue of obedience. He had everything to learn about herding, but once he discovered that he would be helping and pleasing his master, he learned with patience and zeal. A direction once understood was never forgotten, and he went beyond simple obedience:

"When hard pressed in accomplishing the task that he was put to, he had expedients of the moment that bespoke a great share of the reasoning faculty". On one farm where Hogg was shepherd, he had seven hundred lambs under his care at weaning-time. They were of a rebellious breed, and one midnight "the lambs broke and came up the moor upon us, making a noise with their running louder than thunder". Any attempt to turn them back only excited them more; they ran off in three divisions, north, south and west.

"Sirrah, my man, they're a' awa' ", Hogg cried, and Sirrah acted.

In the long night the shepherd and his herd-laddie searched, but lost all the lambs. There seemed nothing for it but to return to the farm and tell their master. On the way, they saw some lambs at the foot of a ravine, safe and sound, guarded by Sirrah, looking round for help but "standing true". Coming nearer, they found it was the whole flock, not one missing. From midnight until sunrise, Sirrah had been alone and undirected. He had found them all.

"If all the shepherds in the Forest had been there to assist him, they could not have effected it with greater propriety".—The word "propriety" is apt; a good dog acts with propriety, in the proper manner, obeys the rules.

Another exploit, hardly less namely, concerned one ewe, a wild one, perverse and foolish, that strayed far from home. Hogg found her fifteen miles away, at Stanhope in Tweeddale, and had to bring her home by a rough track through deep glens and by steep hills. The three of them, man, dog and ewe set out early in the morning:

"She was as wild as a roe, and bounded away to the side of the mountain like one." Sirrah was put in charge, on a wide circle around her. All that day Hogg himself seldom had a sight of her, and at one point lost all trace even of Sirrah and could hear no report of him; until in the evening, on the hillside above Manor Water he came upon his "trusty, coal-black friend" sitting quietly, with eyes fixed on the ewe, with only a glance behind him to see whether his master might be coming. They came safely home together, but when the ewe was set among the flock Sirrah was deeply and justly offended. She ought to have been punished. All that evening at supper he would not speak to his master or eat his food.

Sirrah had another talent. He loved music, especially, as befitted a good Border dog, that of the metrical psalms. "Sacred music affected him most." It drew him irresistibly, and once drawn, he joined in. He had "an outrageous ear" and "many a good psalm, song or tune was he the means of spoiling". Once he joined his voice to others "at which he was not slack", all those others failed. The old farmer, Hogg's master, used prudently to drive Sirrah out to the fields and close the door before he began family worship. Merely to turn him out was not enough; Sirrah went no further than the peat-stack by the door, and there "he did give his powers of voice full scope, without mitigation". He meant well, and could not resist his noble impulses.

Sirrah's end was sad. He was growing old, a son of his was coming on well. Hogg sold him to another shepherd. But Sirrah resented this banishment; he was ready to harm, not to guard the new, strange flock. His new master, in wisdom and kindness, brought him to his old father to be cared for and cherished, "for the sake of what he had been". But something in him was broken, and Hogg never ceased to regret it, never forgot his own unkindness, never again sold an old dog.

One shepherd with a good dog can do more than twenty men without dogs. "Without the shepherd's dog, the whole of the open mountainous land in Scotland would not be worth a six-pence." He is a breadwinner, and he is a character, an individual. Training and discipline do not subdue or flatten personality. Sirrah's son was less valuable, less intelligent than his sire, but he had "three times more humour and whim", besides being docile, patient and true. He had inherited the paternal passion for music, and further enlivened family worship by barking furiously before the end of the prayer.

The Ettrick Shepherd has left the most vivid portraits and paid the greatest tribute to the sheep-dog:

"Neither hunger, fatigue, nor the worst of treatment will drive him from his [master's] side; he will follow him through fire and water . . . through every hardship, without murmur or reproach. . . . Though naturally proud and high-spirited, in so far as relates to his master these qualities . . . are kept so much in subordination that he has not a will of his own".

The relation between man and dog is close, intricate and subtle. All the time, from the first dealing with a collie pup to the moment of triumph at the Sheep Dog Trials, or the still greater triumph of rescue, by both together, of the flock from snow clad hills, there must be perfect mutual trust, respect and understanding, an affection deeper than any sentimentality; and generosity.

There must be no fuss, scolding or impatience. To discipline a puppy needs self-discipline in his master. It is truly an education which develops every resource in the dog of inherited instinct and intelligence.

This is very well shown in that capital story by Kathleen Fidler: *Flash, the Sheep Dog* which is set on a Border farm. Young Tom, coming to live with his aunt and uncle is, at first, lost and bewildered; then, being given for his own, this Border collie pup, he begins a new, full life. His uncle tells him what must not be done: no feeding from the table, no foolish petting, but no scolding, no thrashing. A dog must have scope, must, as Scott said, run in merry circles, but must learn to come to heel; when being led he must not strain on the lead, nor must he be dragged. At all times a word, or a motion of the stick must be enough.

The dog, for his part, must not fuss, scold or bully the sheep. It is a poor dog that rushes at them, barking wildly. The first lesson is to learn to move slowly, crouchingly, toward the sheep, compelling them gently to move as the shepherd bids. Flash learns this; he learns, after Tom has learned how to direct him, to make a cast: to run round behind the flock in a wide half-circle, first to one side, then to the other, and so swerve them towards the shepherd.

Any impatience of word or gesture, even of mood in the man would infect the dog, and, through him, the sheep. Few words are needed; unchanging words: "Come by"; "Bring them out".

A dog should not bark at the sheep; his bark should be his appeal to his master, to ask for his help, call his attention, tell him something. A task done badly must be done again, an excited young dog calmed down; work well done must be rewarded, praise given briefly but warmly. A word is enough. For the mature dog the highest reward is the knowledge of work shared and completed with his master.

Flash in the story proves his good lineage by his quickness in learning, by his quietness and patience, and by his eye; he has the compelling gaze of the true sheepdog.

Before winter comes he is so well trained that he helps to rescue the sheep from the snowdrifts. He had learned how to protect them, too, against attack; he joins the hunt against a marauding fox.

As a puppy he is registered in the Sheep Dog Society; as he progresses, he is entered for the Trials, finally, for the Championship, and this to the joy of the reader, as well as of Tom and his uncle, he wins. Good breeding and good training have their reward. Flash is specially commended for his quietness.

Dogs like men are mortal, and they are prone to the ills of the body, the most serious being hereditary blindness. For any dog this is sad enough, and many are dim of eye long before strength of body has waned; but for the domestic dog it need not be the end of life or joy; he can be protected, he may still have quick hearing and sense of smell. For the sheep-dog to do his work properly, there must be keenness of eye.

There is still a worse deterioration: that of the spirit. It is a noble breed, but even in the noblest there can be a break. An old dog grown useless through lack of strength or sight is pitiful; utterly tragic is one that has become a worrier, an attacker of the sheep he ought to guard. The fox is an open enemy to be met and destroyed; it is his nature to hunt and kill. For a sheepdog this is perversion; he has become a traitor. Mercifully such tragedy is rare.

In March, 1967, *Scotland's Magazine* published an article by Matt Mundell on "Cleeks, Bonnets and the Faithful Collie"— the cleek being the shepherd's crook. He writes, as Hogg did, about suitable names; they should be short: "names that can be shouted quietly and effortlessly through the worst of winter's blizzards and mists, high on the bleak slopes and moorlands";

The Junction Pool of the Tweed at Kelso

names like Corrie, Tweed, Mist, Glen, Sweep, Tam, Cap, Roy
and Will; none of your frivolous fancies.

Sheep Dog Trials are coming near their centenary. The first
was held in Wales, at Bala, in 1873. The Welsh hills make good
training ground, the Welsh collie is a good breed; but it was a
Scot that won.

The great sheep dogs and their owners come from many
parts. In Ayrshire, there was Alexander Millar of Highbowhill,
whose son Jim continues the tradition at Dalry. But for this
narrative it is the Border men and dogs that count.

In the first quarter of this century there was William Wallace
of Otterburn who twice won the international championship,
and whom many experts regard as the pioneer in a new style of
training, a new pattern of trial. There is Jim Wilson, too, with
his dog Roy, formerly of Whitehope on Leithen Water. Also in
Peeblesshire, that county of great dogs, there have been David
Murray's Vic, and John Richardson's Wiston Cap; he was the
youngest dog to win the international title—in 1965. Beyond
Tweedside, though not far away, at Roslin in Midlothian John
Gilchrist and his Spot are famous.

Matt Mundell compares these two, Cap and Spot: "the top
dogs of today in Scotland". Spot is swift though not "flashy",
quick in the uptake as all good sheep dogs must be: "He has a
steady follow after the sheep". Cap is a big dog, eager, alert,
"his ears throughout are always cockit", and he is remarkable
for the width of his sweep when bringing in the sheep.

The breed is still strong, the tradition very much alive.

A Border newspaper records the sheep dog trials held at
Smailholm on 1st July: sixty competitors, some of the sheep
difficult to "lift" and to "drive", but not too difficult for good
dogs and their masters. They came from Peebles and Jedburgh,
from Langholm and Kelso, Lauder, St. Boswells, Greenlaw; the
list would make a map of the Borders. Douglas Lamb of Howden,
Gifford was first, with his dog Glen, J. Richardson of Lyne,
Peebles, close behind him. In the novice class came first of the
entrants Peter Hetherington of Langholm with his Lad who must
have been a proud dog that day.

Another summer event was the visit of two champion sheep-
shearers, both New Zealanders (Brian Quinn and Peter Lincott)
who showed their wonderful skill at Hawick, and were in turn

Tweed-weaving, Galashiels

shown, at a famous mill, the varied use to which the shorn wool is put. So the pattern of life on the Borders continues: the sheep at pasture, the lambing, the shearing; the making of the wool into good "cleiding" both strong and fine; the work of man and dog together in herding the flock, and their hour of triumph at the Trials.

The relation between master and dog has been analysed by a Border shepherd, now living in retirement; Tom Todd, who writes, in prose and in good Scots verse, as T. T. Kilbucho. The relation is nearly always happy, trustful, affectionate; when it breaks down it is more often the fault of the human than of the canine temper. Impatience, anger, unreasonable demands cannot bring forth a full response of obedience, still less of intelligent co-operation. To thrash a collie is both cruel and unnecessary; the average dog is sufficiently rebuked, even shamed by a sharp word.

How intelligent his service can be is shown by more than one recollection. A shepherd one day was planning with another the gathering of the sheep, next morning, for the dipping. When the time came, his old dog was missing, and he set out with a young one. But before they had gone far they met the old dog, bringing in the sheep. He had seen no need to await direct orders.

A rival in sagacity discovered, while the ewes were being clipped, that three were missing. At once he set out to collect them from a mile or two away. By the time their absence had been noted and reported to their master, the dog had brought them in, guided them through the ranks of their shorn sisters, and seen that all was well done.

T. T. Kilbucho has had more than one great dog. In his young days he had one, Rodger, who, as far as work was concerned, was a one-man dog; but in leisure was most sociable. He liked to come "ben the hoose" or into the parlour with his master, lie on the rug by the fire, and listen intelligently to the talk, all but joining in.

Years later, until very recently, there was another Rodger. When he died, full of years, he left a desolation—and a dream:

> Amazin' dogs—since noo I've nane,
> Life canna but hae less for me;
> While ev'n June, wi' Rodger gane,
> Has nae 'er former joys tae gie.

Yet noo an' then the dawn reveals
  The ragged lines o' Rodger still,
Afore a swirlin' mist conceals
  His image ow'r a distant hill.

Many a shepherd must have seen many such a beloved phan-
tom. If ghosts haunt the Borders, as seems not merely credible
but inevitable from the vitality of those who, through the centuries have lived there, and from the strength of their love for
their ain countrie, then the great dogs must be among them:
warriors and reivers on their swift horses, lovers riding together,
the Sheriff away up into the glens and hills of Teviotdale, in
search of ballads, or coming doucely home to Abbotsford, a
shepherd and his collie bringing home the flock—they all live
and move behind the swirl of mist on the Border hills.

X

THE BATTLE OF THE BORDERS, 1966-72

March, march, Ettrick and Teviotdale,
Why the deil dinna ye march forward in order?
March, march, Eskdale and Liddesdale,
All the Blue Bonnets are bound for the Border.
                              —Scott, *The Monastery*

THE Border Development Scheme blew up in 1966 after the issue of a White Paper by the Government; it was a proposal by the Roxburgh County Council to "re-zone" (a jargon word) some 275 acres of land between Melrose and Abbotsford making that area the site for 1,000 houses and industrial buildings. In July, the plan went to the Council; it was passed by a committee; and later in the year it burst upon the public.

The flames of controversy broke out and are still from time to time raging, in the press, in public meetings and in private discussion which is free from restraints and inhibitions. The scheme would, its defenders declared, benefit Galashiels and after that the whole area, by bringing new industry and new people. Its opponents preferred the word "destroy" as regards Melrose and Abbotsford.

The area had previously been "zoned" (in plain English "described") as one "of great landscape value", (or just plain lovely) and thus essential to the life of the Borders. The result of the development would be the end of Melrose as a distinctive country town, the end of pastoral peace, and that is not merely a sentimental objection. This is pastoral country with, in one part, a herd of prize cattle, and in the rest the sheep that, on the Borders, are among the best friends of man. Whether or not the legend is true of Roman or British gold underneath the grass, there is still wealth there, as the sheep graze and flourish.

The plan was to build 1,000 houses by 1970, 9,000 or 10,000 by 1980 with factories to employ some 25,000 people, all within a circuit of fifteen miles. Even without sentimental and anti-quarian argument, without a deep love of the landscape and the character of the countryside, there is the valid plea that this is too great a concentration on one area. The whole Border country needs development, and this should be spread so widely as to help every town. Jedburgh needs help, Hawick could take more.

But the need, now more urgent than ever, for unspoiled country as a refuge from the towns, from noise and pressure of urban life, is also valid. Together both arguments are formidable.

In November there was a spate of letters to the press, from lovers of Scott and of the Scott country, from people in Melrose and its neighbourhood, and from many others who knew and loved that region. In Melrose itself there was a public meeting which came near boiling point. An Edinburgh journalist put it in a well-mixed metaphor (which can be an admirable thing): "It is primarily the site—between Melrose Abbey and Sir Walter Scott's Abbotsford—which has raised Border hackles to the boil." The simmering continues, even if the Blue Bonnets are not marching forth.

There is no opposition to the idea of development, to new industry, to incoming workers. The need for all that is realised. There is strong opposition to this particular site, to the manner of thrusting the scheme upon the neighbourhood: "not only an insult to Scott's memory, but a knife-thrust at Scotland's national pride" as one objector put it. There is the opposition to paper rule, to faceless authority.

The battle has continued ever since the autumn of 1966. In the press, the flood of letters ebbed then flowed again. In January 1967 *The Scotsman* published one from Robert Graves far off in Mallorca defending the region as: "one of the most beautiful and historically holy stretches of country in Scotland. . . . Hundreds of years of poetic influence in the Darnick-Abbotsford district, as yet unspoilt, must not be cut short by inept legislation".

The legislators and their supporters had their say also. Lord Haig of Bemersyde ("Tyde what may betyde...") had a touching faith in the team of planners in Edinburgh and their power to retain the old beauty and peace. To some it appeared ill-omened that these planners had their headquarters in George Square, that once comely place of Georgian houses, built in harmony without exact similarity, set round a garden; Scott's home in boyhood and until his marriage. His house, thanks to careful and watchful owners, and many of the houses on that side of the Square are still unspoiled; but others have been destroyed, and on other sides have arisen sky-scraping towers built by the University. But enough of this bitter loss:

Lord Haig added that there was a plan for planting trees and "landscaping" the area—some might think that the landscape was already there, had long been there, and was of a charm and grace that could not be embellished. The letter ended:

"Though the opinions of expatriate Scots and interested, eminent writers from places like Mallorca would be valuable, it would be a mistake to allow them to hamper the *natural evolution* of the Borders. We cannot be sacrificed as a kind of museum piece with our minds focussing inwards and on the past."

The two words italicised are, to the mind of the objectors to the plan, false and absurd; the proposed development seems to them neither natural nor an evolution; it is an imposition. To picture the Borderers gazing dreamily into the past, seated among picturesque ruins of crumbling abbeys, hollow oaks and all the rest of it, is to have a singularly ill-focused and unclear vision of them.

The planners were vigorously defended, their opponents attacked by the chairman of Pringle's of Hawick (Mr. McTaggart), who deplored "the hysterical outbursts of what I am convinced (and nearly everyone else is convinced) is a mere handful of people . . . a noise out of all proportion to the general feeling of the whole community."

A handful? It rather depends on the size of the hand, which could be a gigantic one.

A further argument (by Lord Haig) for the development was that the area to be built with houses and factories and a new bridge over Tweed (was this one foreseen by True Thomas?) would be "a vital component of Galashiels", a focal point. Against this, Andrew Haddon of Hawick argued cogently, asking whence the "labour catchment" of some 73,000 people would be drawn to fill the new houses and factories. Had the site been properly surveyed? It was prone to floods. Lord Stratheden and Campbell replied that the people would come from burghs and villages within fifteen miles of Galashiels. The site, admittedly, had not been fully surveyed, because it was still private land. One party of surveyors had been told, by the owner, to leave, and had done so. How they were told is, regrettably, not reported, but it was probably in good plain English, not jargon.

Then Robin McEwen of Marchmont in Berwick joined the protestors, deprecating the "linear expansion" as a mere sprawl. The result would be "a sprawling new town in the Borders, against the present interests, the future prospects and the past traditions of every Border burgh and village". There was left in the mind an "ignoble vision" of a garden city, suitable perhaps for the home counties, for suburban country, as a dormitory, no longer a living place.

In February, the Tweed Valley Association (of the protestors) sent a letter to all the Roxburgh County Councillors urging them to think again upon this development, and recalling the history of the plan. The scheme set forth in the Government White Paper of January 1966 was for "re-zoning" 275 acres between Darnick and Abbotsford for 1,000 houses and for factories. This had been passed by the local committee in July, but returned to them in November, by the full Council, after a dispute on procedure. The proposal was emended, reducing the area for building by twenty acres and setting aside a part for "landscaping". This was approved by the County Convener, Lord Stratheden and Campbell.

The Tweed Valley Association, having small faith in the "equivocations and unenforceable assurances" of the Council, pointed out that the plan would not develop existing small communities, but would merely link Galashiels with St. Boswell's, perhaps with Kelso, while draining other towns. They were sceptical about the "landscaping", about the promise to produce "a park-like setting". Their faith in planning officials was limited.

All their objections were over-ruled by the County Council, as was their proposal to have the matter deferred for eleven months, until the whole Government plan for the Borders was made known.

Speaking for the Council and the planners, Professor Johnson-Marshall of Edinburgh University, their consultant, insisted on the creation of a garden-city, the continuance of village life;

people would still live in their villages and travel to work in the towns. This was denied by the Provost of Kelso who thought that the small communities would decay and disintegrate.

The plan by this time was to "re-zone" 147 acres, and "to inject 25,000 [people] into the Western Borders by 1980".

The Planning Convener, Councillor Stevenson, criticised the Association's letter as inaccurate, and thought it "should be treated with the respect it deserves which is to ignore it". The plan was for "linear development" which would link communities "through an area of high amenity", not for "ribbon development" along main roads. (Any query about the difference would, no doubt, be treated "with the respect it deserves, which is to ignore it") The plea for delay was refused because it would give industrialists a bad impression of Roxburgh as "a half-hearted, fuddy-duddy old county which is not worth coming to. If we delay again, then I am afraid for our name in this county".

About the same time *The Scotsman* published, in a page of articles about regional development, two concerning the Borders. Mr. T. D. Thomson, Honorary Secretary of the Eastern Borders Development Association, dealt with that region which includes northern Northumberland, Berwick, Kelso, and parts of Berwickshire and Roxburghshire. It is, superficially, one of good farms, of fisheries on the coast, of small towns with good family business firms, and with plenty of tourism in summer; but "in fact we have been bleeding to death for most of this century"—at least since the 1914–18 war with its catastrophic loss of manhood. Employment has been reduced—by increase of mechanism on the farms, decrease of railways, amalgamation of schools, of medical and other services. It would seem the point of no return.

There was much local concern over this, but not enough national awareness. The departure of the young, especially of men, south of the Border and overseas made unemployment appear less of a problem than it really was. Complacency and defeatism, although opposite faults could unite to prevent development.

The Eastern Development Association was formed in 1961 between local authorities and leaders of commerce and industry. They must deal with two problems—depopulation and unemployment; and had prepared an integrated programme of social and economic development, including the building of factories in Berwick and Kelso. The Development Committee was to employ a full time officer with an office in Berwick.

Help was given by the Rural Industries Bureau and the Scottish Country Industries Development Trust. There was much need for more work, more opportunities for young people, just leaving school, more work altogether within the region, more use of such natural resources as the water of Tweed, more money for every town. Jobs were not enough; there must be good houses, good public services, good social life with attractions for tourists.

For the Western Borders, Mr. Ernest Tait, Chairman of the Border Economic Planning Consultative Group (one is slightly awed by the magnitude of these titles) wrote approving the plans in the White Paper: "some of the most important and far-reaching which have been made for the present and future welfare of Scotland and Scotsmen". The Darnick–Abbotsford plan was commended. He urged the activity of consultative groups with a team of expert consultants. Everything must be surveyed: housing, labour resources, industries, railways.

This writer was, on the whole, optimistic. There would be "a healthy upsurge" of life and prosperity in the future; but the Borders have to compete with other regions in attracting both industry and tourism; Borderers must be active, progressive, and forget their "parochialism".

But this is what some lovers of the Borders would call independence, distinctiveness between one town and another. They have been different, each from the other, for a long time, they have their strong local tradition and loyalty.

The Tweed Valley Association and all who are with them in detesting and opposing the Darnick–Abbotsford scheme are very far from denying the need for new industry, new opportunity, new life; they only cannot see how this particular bit of a plan is constructive or creative.

In one of the Border newspapers (*The Southern Reporter*) Mr. Tait described the Darnick–Melrose–Abbotsford plan as "reasonable, well-balanced and capable of being made an attractive proposal", of becoming "an attractive and desirable little township or extension to Galashiels without damaging any of the existing beauties".

To this the objectors might well reply: let Galashiels have its extension to it reserved; let the township be built on that side of the river, beyond the town. And from other Border towns has come the objection that this scheme will not help them in their need for growth.

At a dinner of the Hawick Angling Club, usually a peaceful occasion, for anglers above all sportsmen are men of peace, of mellow words and few, Lord Haig hit out at the objectors: "To my mind the area chosen is not of major visual significance. The banks of the Tweed are not being affected, and the selected area is relatively tucked away."

The battle continued and local criticism of the proposals became intensified. At a meeting in Melrose the plan was again attacked by Professor Hugh Trevor-Roper, the historian, who lives in Melrose, declaring that even with good building and lay-out of landscaping, the whole place would be changed for the worse. Not only was it a place of beauty but one of pilgrimage, "a devotional scene" unrivalled in its associations. As such it drew visitors from all over the world.

He further criticised the White Paper as an expression of "panic haste", of publishing only the first part of a development as yet unknown or at least undescribed. The whole had not been told to the people most concerned.

This objection was emphasised by Mr. A. T. McIndoe, a town planning consultant of long experience. The Darnick–Melrose–Abbotsford plan had been chosen not as the best but as the easiest: "There is an increasing tendency in planning to pick the easiest area with the best amenity and the least trouble".

The planners had concentrated on one way of solving the problem of depopulation: that of injecting or "pumping 25,000 people" rapidly, into one area, of thrusting city families into a rural setting which would mean a different way of life. The admittedly difficult question of holding, by new industry and employment, the existing population, had not been sufficiently studied.

From many meetings, many objections, much correspondence it is clear that local resentment is primarily and essentially against the violent thrusting of the White Paper and the Plan upon the people most intimately concerned, against the cloudiness which surrounds possible or probable developments.

A new suggestion has been made: that there be co-operation between Planning Commissions in a wide area, Solway as well as Tweed, and on both sides of the Border.

In June 1967 the Darnick inquiry held at Melrose, into the proposed scheme, ended with a ruling by the Reporter, Sir Robert Russell, that a document dealing with an alternative site should not be held confidential—as was argued by the County Clerk of Selkirk. Speaking for the objectors to the plan, Mr. Robert Reid, Q.C., criticised the Secretary of State for Scotland for intervention and lack of impartiality. The result of this was the profound feeling of bitterness among the objectors, their sense that a decision had been made without their knowledge, without any consultation with them.

So, for four years, the matter has rested. Whatever the issue, however long or short the struggle, the end cannot lack bitterness. Victory will be resented by the defeated. There is more than a sentimental conservatism here more than local and parochial antagonism. The feeling goes very deep: love of a landscape, of a tradition, a sense of fitness, a resistance to alien invasion, to any form of stampeding. All these lie within and behind the opposition.

Comment has been made in verse:

> True Thomas lay on Huntlie bank,
>   A ferlie he spied wi' his e'e;
> For there he saw a muckle pack
>   O' planners spread owre the countrie.
>
> And on they rade, and on they cam'
>   By fair Melrose to Abbotsford;
> And wi' them Haig o' Bemersyde,
>   And (Losh behears!) a Campbell lord!
>
> True Thomas spak': "Fu' mony a doom
>   Ha'e I foreseen wi' mony a tear,
> But ne'er sae black a thing I saw
>   As what thae loons are plannin' here".
>
> To him then answered Michael Scott
>   The mighty warlock: "Tam, my man,
> We ken some magic, it behoves
>   Us ding them doun, them and their plan;

"You wi' your harp, I wi' my book
   May weave a spell to stay their haun's".
"Aye", said True Thomas, "that we will.
   While Tweed rins deep and Eildon staun's

"In triple peak, they'll come na near
   The place whaur dwalt Sir Walter Scott:
A minstrel he, and wizard gude!
   He loo'ed us, and we'll foil their plot".

———

As this new edition goes to press the planners appear to have won the campaign, although their opponents are unlikely to accept defeat meekly. The Roxburgh County Council, meeting in November, voted by a majority of 37 to resume the Tweedbank Development Scheme which had been delayed for four years by legal action, now ended, on the part of one landowner. Meanwhile the cost of development had risen from £10 million to over £13 million. Work, it was decided, should begin within a month. One speaker dwelt hopefully on the large amount of money to be spent within the county, the prospect of employment, the new opportunities. Another pointed out gloomily that the delay had meant loss; three firms had already withdrawn. There was some argument between the burghs as to whether Galashiels or the whole county should bear the expense in added rates. It was argued that the whole matter should be considered not from a local point of view, not even from that of the borders alone, but from that of all Scotland. The county convener, the Duke of Roxburghe, declared that to turn the plan down now would be to become "the laughing-stock of the nation".

There are other opinions, still being lucidly expressed. Walking in the grounds of Abbotsford on a November afternoon, one realises that only a field and a new plantation of trees will divide Scott's home and land from the new road leading to the new bridge over Tweed, and beyond the road the settlement of new houses on the way to Melrose.

XI

BORDERERS AND THEIR HOMES

It is perhaps rather hard on other Border clans than Scott, on Kerrs, Douglases, Homes and others that they have produced no major genius, although they have provided from time to time both the persons and the subjects of ballad and legend. There is a Scott country, but not, except in local speech, a Kerr or other region. For all that, there are many notable personalities and families, some of them still dwelling in their ancestral home.

Kelso is in Kerr or Ker country, and on the outskirts of the town is one of the grandest of Border mansions, Floors Castle, the home of the Duke of Roxburghe; it is said to be the largest inhabited house in Scotland. It was designed in 1718 by Vanbrugh, for the first Duke, enlarged and remodelled between 1838 and 1849 by Playfair, and is altogether palatial. The Duke is twelfth in succession and descends from Sir Robert Ker of Cessford who in 1600 was created Lord Roxburghe, and in 1616 Lord Ker of Cessford and Earl of Roxburghe. The fifth Earl was made Duke, with the secondary title of Marquess of Bowmont which is borne by the Duke's heir. The family name is Innes-Ker, the Innes having come in by marriage.

There are Kerrs also at Monteviot, Ancrum, near Jedburgh. Their head is the Marquess of Lothian who descends from Mark Kerr of Cessford, created Earl of Lothian in 1606, and from another Kerr, Andrew of Ferniehurst who, in the previous century had married Janet Hume of Polwarth; their son married a Kerr of Cessford. They became Kerrs of Ancram and the Earldom, having lapsed in the Cessford line was renewed in this. In Mary Stuart's reign Sir Thomas Kerr was one of her devoted adherents; his younger son, by his marriage with Janet Kirkcaldy of Grange, took his mother's name, and as Kirkcaldy of Grange was one of the most notorious of those nobles who surrounded the unhappy Queen. There was a later alliance with the Humes of Polwarth when a daughter of the Kerrs, Julian, married Sir Patrick Hume, and, being widowed, married again, the first Earl of Haddington, a Hamilton. This, three great Border names, Kerr, Hume, Hamilton are interwoven, as Hume and Hamilton will be in another family. The pattern of descent, marriage and kinship in the great Border families is too intricate to be set forth in detail, except in the pages of Burke and Debrett, but even a glimpse of it has interest.

The first Earl of Lothian—in the revived title borne by Kerr of Ancram, was raised to the Marquessate; the title Earl of Ancram is now borne by the eldest son. In the nineteenth century there was a marriage with the Scotts of Buccleuch and one with the English Talbots. The seventh Marquess married Lady Cecil Talbot whose charming Christian name recurs in the family. In her devout Anglican days she helped to build the Episcopal church of St. John, in Jedburgh; after her conversion to Rome she, with the Hope-Scotts, had much to do with the building of the Catholic church there, and with Catholic life in the Borders.

The present Marquess, the twelfth in line, succeeded a kinsman in 1940. The succession has more than once been continued through cousins. The eleventh Marquess, before his succession, was Philip Kerr who had a distinguished career as statesman and diplomat; he was Under Secretary of State for India from 1931–32, and Ambassador to Washington from 1939–40. A still more eminent member of the family in that generation was Admiral Mark Kerr who to his great naval services added that of helping to form the Royal Air Force, who took to flying as he did to the sea, was author as well as pioneer-airman, and by gallantry and versatility a true and complete Borderer.

The present Marquess has served as delegate to the General Assembly of United Nations and as United Kingdom Delegate to the Council of Europe. In the last Conservative Government he was Parliamentary Private Secretary to the Secretary of State for Foreign Affairs, and later Joint Parliamentary Secretary to the Ministry of Health.

Perhaps the loveliest, certainly the most elegant mansion on the Borders is Mellerstain which lies between Gordon in Berwickshire and Kelso, just within the boundaries of the Scott country.

It is the home of the Earl of Haddington whose family name is
Baillie-Hamilton and who has a double kinship with the Kerrs
of Lothian; both descend from Humes of Polwarth, and Julian
Kerr married *en second noces*, an Earl of Haddington.

His most famous and delightful ancestress is Lady Grisell
Baillie, born Grisell Hume, daughter of Sir Patrick of that name
who in 1696 was Lord Chancellor of Scotland and became Lord
Polwarth, and later, Earl of Marchmont. In that last decade of
the seventeenth century he was in great honour and prosperity,
under William and Mary, but ten years earlier he had been a
hunted man, an ardent Presbyterian, under the ban of James
VII and II. For a while he lay hidden in the tower of the church
near his house. His daughter Grisell used to smuggle food to
him. The secret was known only to a few, and was wisely kept
from the younger children. One day at dinner they had sheep's
head broth, from which Grisell contrived to extract the sheep's
head, hiding it under her apron, to be taken to her father. A small
brother noticed its disappearance without suspecting the reason:
"Mother will you look at Grisell", he exclaimed. "While we
were supping our broth, she has eaten a whole sheep's head".

In time, Sir Patrick escaped with his family to Holland where
they lived in exile, safe but impoverished, their domestic affairs
excellently managed by Grisell, until William of Orange went
to England, pushed his father-in-law King James off the throne,
and sat himself thereon. The Humes and other Scots exiles
returned with him, among them young George Baillie of Jervis-
wood and Mellerstain to whom Grisell had become betrothed.
Theirs is one of the true romances of history; their marriage one
of profound happiness clouded only by the death in childhood
of their only son, Robin. Two daughters were left to them,
Grisell and Rachel.

George Baillie and Lady Grisell (as she became on the eleva-
tion of her father to the Earldom of Marchmont) lived in London,
in Edinburgh and at Mellerstain; not in the house we see today
but in a smaller mansion which had its own elegance and charm
and which this most notable of housewives delighted to furnish.
Her Household Books are not only a family treasure, they are
an incomparable source of material for social and domestic
history.

Now in her days of wealth as in her earlier poverty she kept accounts carefully: for building and upkeep of house and estate, for wages, for food and furniture, dress for herself and her daughters, for their music and dancing lessons, for a multitude of details including a brush for the dog. She also wrote down recipes and dinner menus from her own parties and those given by friends and neighbours, usually with a plan of the table and a list of guests.

Hers is the most entrancing of domestic chronicles and the most revealing; she emerges from those domestic items as clearly as from any journal, she reveals herself—practical, domestic, capable, authoritative, indulgent as a mother, strict as the mistress of a great house. Her affection for her little daughters has a gentleness and gaiety unusual in that age of discipline of the young. She loved to buy pretty things for them, and her daughter Grisell, Lady Murray, who left a memoir of her parents, records the same indulgence in her father. He used to come home from London with his valise stuffed with presents.

There never was a greater lady and there never was one who was less of a "fine lady" in the insipid sense of the term than Lady Grisell. To choose a few items from her Accounts:

"To mending old Ditch Dick in Coltcrooks" may sound puzzling. Who was this old Dick and what had they done to him to send him into the ditch and need mending? The translation is—ditch dyke or fence. The use of capitals is misleading if beguiling, and Lady Grisell like most of her contemporaries, however highly educated, spelled more or less as she chose. The cost of mending Ditch Dick was tenpence. There are many payments for repairs, for upkeep of fields, fences and houses. Mellerstain had many windows, but at twopence halfpenny each they may not have been too costly a repair. There are many items of furniture: tables, chairs, some rush-bottomed, one "buffed" or padded easy-chair (this by no means a usual luxury) a fixed bed for the nursery; quantities of hangings for the beds; screens, bookcases, one with a looking-glass door; the equipage of the tea-table, and tea which at the beginning of the eighteenth century was a costly drink, sometimes at twenty shillings a pound.

Mellerstain saw many guests, and there are many bills of fare to show what they ate for dinner or supper; the former meal was then served in the afternoon. It consisted of two courses and dessert, but the courses were each ample and varied enough to be a meal in themselves. The custom of serving each kind of food separately and successively, through soup, fish, meat and so on to dessert is no earlier than Victorian. Until then, the dinner table was set with a variety of dishes, the first course removed to make way for the second at which both savoury and sweet dishes appeared with vegetables and other accompaniments. Dessert was a fairy feast of delicacies.

One of Lady Grisell's suppers included salmon, collops, lobsters, ducklings, roast chickens, fricassee of calves feet, and a ragout of hare, followed by jellies, ratafia cream, possets, syllabubs and lemon hatted kit. Syllabub is a delectable mixture of cream and wine, posset rather more substantial, with eggs "intil't", hatted kit a junket of sweet and butter milk together. A Christmas dinner offered roast beef and chicken as first course, with plum pudding and its ancestor plum (which she spells plumb) potage, made with sago and fruit, and mince pies; followed, as second course, by roast goose, tongue, wildfowl and "oyster loves" or loaves or patties. Finally came the exquisite dessert of syllabub, creams, jellies, fruit and nuts. One of Lady Grisell's favourite devices was a dish of stewed or preserved apples or pears with fresh ones round.

What strikes the modern reader is not only the lavishness but the variety. This was, of course, a rich house; the poor lived meagrely. But here we find not only an ample supply of meat and other solid food, but of vegetables, fruit, and preserves. Stillroom cookery was an important part of the domestic economy, and the stillroom cupboards held many delights.

The staff who cooked those meals and washed up afterwards, who kept the house in cleanliness and comfort were well disciplined. Both housekeeper and butler were given their precise duties and responsibilities, and were enjoined to rise early in order to set their underlings about their work.

"Keep the maids close at their spinning till nine at night, when they are not washing or at other necessary work" Lady Grisell told her housekeeper; and to her butler: "Consider your business and have a little forethought that you may never be in a hurry or have anything to seek."

Stores must be carefully given out. The servants' sheets were changed once a month; as for the family laundry—bed linen and personal linen were washed in alternate weeks. The servants had their rations, including beer; no tea which was still a drink for the gentry. On Sunday they had boiled beef for dinner with the broth in which it had been boiled; on Monday, broth and herring, on Tuesday broth and beef, on Wednesday broth and eggs, Thursday broth and beef, Friday broth and herring, Saturday broth with cheese or pudding. This was their dinner. For breakfast and supper they had oaten or wheaten bread with milk or beer. One strict rule was that there must be "no santering [sauntering] odd people come about the house"—none of the servants' poor relations, no hopeful hangers-on or vagrants, only "those that have business, and that not a meal time, which they will always do if not hindered".

In the 1730s the Baillies, their daughters now grown up, made foreign tours, bringing home treasures from France and Italy: busts, medallions, little boxes, silver candlesticks, books of prints and engravings.

Their younger daughter, Rachel, married Lord Binning, son and heir of the Earl of Haddington; he died before his father, and their elder son became Lord Haddington after his grandfather's death. The younger son, George, inherited Mellerstain and assumed the additional surname of Baillie. He would appear to have inherited Lady Grisell's love of beauty, her creative sense of home-making. Mellerstain as it is today is largely his creation, his ideas carried out by William Adam the distinguished father of those still more distinguished sons.

George Baillie-Hamilton travelled much in Europe, cultivating his innate classical taste. His Mellerstain begun by himself and William Adam, continued by Robert Adam, is in a pure classical style and in its richness and perfection of detail would have entranced Lady Grisell.

From the hall a double staircase and barrel-vaulted corridors lead to the main rooms which look out on the wonderful garden. This is like something from a villa in Italy or a château in Touraine; it is landscaped, descending in terraces to a lake, with a most ordered beauty yet not disciplined out of true garden-loveliness. In spring it is a golden sea of daffodils; but every season brings its delights and even in winter there is the unchanging elegance. Much of this is due to the creative care of Lady Haddington.

In the house, as in all Adam houses, there are lovely ceilings, in library, drawing-room and dining-room, moulded like Wedgwood medallions. The study has two ceilings for it has been made out of two small rooms. In the library is a fine mantelpiece of green and white marble.

If ghosts could walk, and one sometimes hopes they may, Lady Grisell's must come often to the house which has grown out of the one she made and loved, the house her grandson, Rachel's son, brought to perfection. Many things would be familiar to her, especially the portraits: her husband George Baillie by Alan Ramsay, her old father by Aikman, Grisell and Rachel her daughters as children, by Scougal, and very formal and grand little ladies they look, dressed for the occasion in the finery which is a minature copy of grownup dress; they have been painted again in their graceful womanhood, Grisell by Alan Ramsay, Rachel by Maria Verelst who has also painted Lady Grisell herself. They are portraits of the characters in a domestic chronicle.

The house holds not only beauty and family records but the intangible atmosphere of family life through the generations. Lady Grisell would feel very much at home, and no doubt go off to the servants' hall and kitchen, to be somewhat bewildered by the lack of the army of servants she had once ruled.

Lord Haddington bears the name of the maker of Mellerstain; he too is George Baillie-Hamilton. He has served in both world wars. After the end of the first, in the early 1920s, he went out to Canada on the staff of the Governor General, the Duke of Devonshire. There he met his bride, Miss Sarah Cook. With him was his friend and fellow Border laird, Lord Minto; he too found his romance there, marrying Lady Haddington's sister, Marion.

The Mintos are Elliot, descending from Gilbert Elliot who was created a Baronet in 1700. His son, the second baronet was father of Jean, the author of "The Floo'ers o' the Forest"; and to her brother must be given a share of the credit for he wagered her she could not write a poem in the style of the old ballads, and she won the bet. The fourth baronet, and first Earl of Minto, was Governor General of Bengal; and the fourth Earl, father of the present peer, was Governor General of Canada, and then Viceroy of India.

Lord Minto gives his recreations as hunting, shooting and fishing; Lord Haddington's are more scholarly. He is President of the Society of Antiquaries of Scotland, President of the

Georgian Society, a Trustee of the National Library of Scotland and of the National Museum of Antiquities. He is most admirably proud of his descent from Lady Grisell. The sister Countesses are notable both for their charm and for their activity in good works in their counties, in the Red Cross and in youth work.

The Mintos live at Braehead near St. Boswells. The family seat, Minto House, at Denholm (that delightful village with its wide green, of a pattern unusual in Scotland) near Hawick was, for some years, a girls' school and is, at the moment, in the market. It is a great mansion with about seventy rooms, and it is said to be haunted. We have Sir Walter Scott's word for this, in his Journal. He reports that the first Earl, the Governor of Bengal, came home with a guilty secret, that he had constructed a suite of hidden rooms to which none but himself knew the access, and that long after his death he haunted the woods around his mansion, at night, in his white beard and a white night-cap. No one has seen him; but no one of any feeling, in Scotland, thinks any the worse of a family that has a secret and a ghost.

The name of Elliot is carried also, and carried vigorously and with panache, by a lady: Baroness Elliot of Harwood near Hawick. She is a life Peeress, and was born a Tennant: Katharine, daughter of Sir Charles Tennant of the Glen, Peeblesshire, half-sister to Margot, Countess of Oxford and Asquith, and to the first Lord Glentanar. Like her sister, she married into politics; her husband was Walter Elliot who, in the Conservative Government of the 1930s held a series of offices culminating in that of Secretary of State for Scotland. At Harwood Lady Elliot farms, (a ram and a horse are the supporters on her coat of arms); she sits on many boards and committees, and is especially interested in Child Welfare. Only two women have been chosen Chairman of the Sir Walter Scott Club of Edinburgh, to give the toast of The Immortal Memory at the annual dinner. One was Lady Tweedsmuir (daughter-in-law of John Buchan) the other Lady Elliot.

Near Hawick, too, is Harden, home of the Scotts of Harden whose head is Lord Polwarth. He shares an ancestor—in Auld Wat of Harden—with Sir Walter Scott and his descendants, and one with Lord Haddington in Sir Patrick Hume who became Lord Polwarth and was father of Lady Grisell; Sir Patrick, as we have seen, was raised to the Earldom of Marchmont, which became extinct on the death of his grandson without male issue. The Lordship of Polwarth continued in the female line, and was carried by marriage into the family of Scott of Harden.

The present descendent of Auld Wat and of Sir Patrick has turned his inherited energy into business and finance. He is a Chartered Accountant, Deputy Governor of the Bank of Scotland, Chairman of the Executive Committee of the Scottish Council of Development and Industry, and holds many directorships. In more traditional and, if you like, romantic manner, he is one of the Queen's Bodyguard for Scotland, the Royal Archers, as are his fellow Border-peers, Lord Haddington and Lord Minto.

The ducal head of the Scotts is the Duke of Buccleuch who has the triple surname of Montagu-Douglas Scott and the other Dukedom of Queensberry—a Douglas one. His heir is the Earl of Dalkeith who lives at Eildon Hall, near Melrose and who is M.P. for Edinburgh North. The Duke's Border mansion is Bowhill, near Selkirk.

The peerage goes back to 1606 when Sir Walter Scott "a powerful chieftain and a military commander of renown in the Netherlands"—according to *Debrett*—was created Lord Scott of Buccleuch; his son was made Earl. The title descended in the female line, and in 1663 Anne, Countess of Buccleuch in her own right, married James, Duke of Monmouth, the most (perhaps the only) luckless one of Charles II's natural sons; they bore the double title of Duke and Duchess of Monmouth and Buccleugh, until, after the death of King Charles, Monmouth raised his ill-fated rebellion against his uncle James VII and II who dealt mercilessly with him. The Duke was executed, his honours and titled attainted; his Duchess was left her own title of Buccleugh and so the succession continued. The third Duke became also the Duke of Queensberry with the surname of Douglas. The third name, Montagu, links the family with that of Montagu of Beaulieu.

The Buccleuchs have given us a Royal Duchess. The Duchess of Gloucester is a sister of the present Duke. The Duke is Governor of the Bank of Scotland, and is President of many agricultural societies and associations. He gives his recreations as farming, forestry and shooting, and the first two may also count as his business and vocation. There is another family mansion in Dumfriesshire, but the Borders claim him as their Duke.

Douglas and Home (pronounced Hume) are intermarried in the lineage of Sir Alec Douglas Home, who in his youth was Lord Dunglass, son and heir to the Earl of Home. He succeeded as fourteenth Earl in 1951 and in 1963 renounced his Earldom for life, to become Sir Alec Douglas Home and lead the Conservative Government as Prime Minister in the House of Commons. Men have claimed a dormant or disputed peerage before now; but such a renunciation as this is unique.

The Douglases go back to Scotland's Wars of Independence, and the Good Lord James lives in heroic tradition along with his King, Robert the Bruce. This family is of the Western Lowlands rather than the East; the Homes are Border stock, Borderers of Borderers. They go back at least to the fourteenth century; one Sir Thomas Home flourished about 1385. The barony dates from the fifteenth century, when another Sir Alexander became the first Lord Home. The third Baron fought at Flodden but his dealings with the English somehow gave rise to the chant of the souters of Selkirk:

"Doun wi' the Earls o' Home"—although the Earldom did not come until the reign of James VI and I.

The tenth Earl married a daughter of the third Duke of Buccleugh and Queensberry; the eleventh married a daughter of Lord Montagu and her mother was a Douglas, daughter of the first Lord Douglas, Archibald Steuart-Douglas about whose inheritance and title hangs one of the most complicated legal tales in Scottish family history. The Douglas Cause was one of the liveliest battles ever waged in even the Scottish Court of Session, and is still famous.

It all began with the marriage, in 1748, of Lady Jane Douglas, sister of the first (and only) Duke of Douglas, to Sir John Steuart, a man of good family but shady reputation, in fact, an adventurer; but a devoted husband enough, and the marriage, though violently disapproved by Lady Jane's brother the Duke, would appear to have been happy. In 1748 Lady Jane wrote to her brother of her hopes of a child; later that year, in Paris, she gave birth to twin sons—or she, her husband and her nurse said she did. Others said that she was past the age of child-bearing, and that the babies were supposititious, the offspring of French peasants. One version is that Lady Jane did really have her babies, who died at birth, and that, to spare her a grief which might have killed her (with, possibly, other motives less amiable) her husband procured those boys.

One of the twins, Sholto, died in childhood, to his mother's intense grief. The other, Archibald, grew to manhood, and is the hero of the Cause. The Duke refused to receive his sister or recognise her son. She died, broken-hearted and in poverty; her husband was in prison for debt. The Duke, like his sister, made a late marriage, a childless one, to a kinswoman, Miss Peggy Douglas of Mains, a most redoubtable lady who took the side of her sister-in-law and of young Archibald. Before he died, the Duke acknowledged the young man as his nephew and heir, settling on him the vast estates he had previously settled on his nearest kinsman otherwise, the young Duke of Hamilton, a Douglas-Hamilton.

On the Duke's death in 1760 the Hamiltons hotly contested Archibald's right to succession, declaring him to be no son of Lady Jane, sending an agent to Paris to discover the facts. The story is too long and complicated to give except in the briefest summary, but it is one of the best thrillers without murder that can be desired.

When the matter was tried before the Court of Session in Edinburgh, the judges—the Fifteen—were divided, seven for Archibald, seven for the Duke of Hamilton; the Lord President gave his casting vote for the Hamiltons. Archibald took his cause to the House of Lords, who overturned the decision of the Court of Session, pronouncing him truly the son of Lady Jane and her husband. This verdict was hailed in Edinburgh with exultance, and the mob, who detested the powerful Hamiltons, broke the windows of the Lord President.

Archibald was not retained in the Dukedom, but became Lord Douglas of Douglas—in 1790, thirty years after the death of the old Duke. He married twice and exaltedly; first a daughter of the Duke of Montrose, second, a daughter of the Duke of Buccleugh, thus strengthening the Douglas name. Of his family of twelve, some of whom died before him, only one, a daughter, left issue; and one of her daughters became Countess of Home.

So we come back to the fourteenth Earl, now Sir Alec. The family history has much variety and some violence, the present generation have variety without violence. There is a diversity of gifts in its head and in his brothers, William the playwright (who has portrayed their father, the thirteenth Earl in one of his diverting comedies) and Henry the naturalist and bird-man. Sir Alec was chairman of the Sir Walter Scott Club in 1967 and made the oration of a good Borderer and lover of the greatest of Borderers. He may be adequately portrayed, some years hence, in biography or memoir, when the dust of political conflict has blown away.

Sir Alec has been interviewed (by *The Weekly Scotsman*) at his home, The Hirsel near Coldstream in Berwickshire, on the southern edge of the Borders, just within the radius of the Scott Country. The gardens are famous for their azaleas and-rhododendrons and for a lake which is a miniature bird sanctuary. Here, in a setting of peace and loveliness hardly changed through the centuries of family history, the former Prime Minister looked back on forty years of political life by no means free from storm and stress, and considered some of the urgencies of today.

There was a hint of a shadow of regret about his renouncing his title: "The final decision to leave the House of Lords required a great deal of thought and heart-searching. I don't know if I was right; anyhow its useless to look backwards."

If no longer Earl of Home he is still a Border laird; and it was the laird who, with his lady, received members of the Sir Walter Scott Club of Edinburgh one evening in early June when the guests felt themselves moving in a timeless world for one enchanted space of time. They came as lovers of Scott into a scene he would have found homely: a country house, gardens beyond, and beyond the gardens the fields and pastures full of life and growth and peace.

Auction ring, August lamb sales, Hawick
(overleaf) *The Valley of the Yarrow, and the castle of Newark*

XII

SPRING ON THE BORDERS

JANUARY 1967 came, behaved and departed in a temperate manner. February began well enough for that unchancy, some would say vicious little month, but ended in gales. Candlemas had perhaps not been a foul enough day.

> If Candlemas be clear and fair,
> The half o' the winter's to come and mair;
> If Candlemas be dull and foul,
> The half of the winter is bye at Yule.

March came in like a lion, as the old phrase describes it, and a bad-tempered lion at that; the roaring was not soon abated, and there was no lamb-like exit.

The lambs themselves were reluctant to be born, and on a March journey into the Borders there were few to be seen in the fields. The spring flowers were hardier and more daring, taking the winds of March with beauty, lighting the dim green of the landscape with brilliant lamps of blue and white and gold. Even in a garden set among the hills there were clusters of crocus, scylla and primrose, and the daffodils came out in time for the early Easter.

But Hawick, on a grey, windy day seemed to be drawing itself together within its encircling hills. There is in any case a concentrated air about Hawick; it minds its business, and there is a good deal of business to mind with famous woollen, hosiery and tweed mills, cleaners and dyers. You may buy a very elegant jersey suit here, and fine blankets and other comforts, and when after grateful wear they are soiled, send them to be expertly cleaned.

The mills and factories are working every day; there is, besides, the regular auction market, the oldest in Britain, still

*The Duke of Buccleuch's hounds arriving at a meet at
Merton, St. Boswell's*

managed by one family after 150 years. Immense numbers of sheep, lambs and cattle are exchanged here. Ponies and hunters are also bought and sold, for this is hunting country. There are six Border hunts. The past winter, being most of the time open weather, was a good season for hunting.

"Hounds ran very fast and with a great cry"—is a sentence from one press report which might well come into a ballad or a legend.

Very much a manufacturing and industrial town, almost like Glasgow in miniature, close-packed of necessity within its frame of hills, with Teviot running alongside and Slitrig joining Teviot, Hawick is at the same time a farming, pastoral and hunting community. If it were not for the sheep on the hills and the strong, running water of the rivers there would be no mills, even if some of the finer wool comes from overseas. If it were not for the sheep and cattle market and for the demand for wool, the farmers would not prosper. Town and country, manufactures and pastoral ways and crafts mingle and are mutually necessary.

It has been a lively winter on the Borders. These towns with their surrounding villages make their own way of life and entertainment still, whatever the spell of television or the lure of the city. Hawick Amateur Dramatic Society presented *Oklahoma*, Melrose produced Gilbert and Sullivan—*The Sorcerers*—St. Boswell's Drama Group played *Cat and the Fiddle*, Selkirk formed a branch of the Scottish National Party. Political feeling is fairly strong, and local elections have their own drama.

Hawick has not (at the moment of writing) decided whether or not to send the cavalcade of their Common Riding to the parade in Edinburgh in August. Galashiels has agreed to join, Selkirk has refused. Hawick Town Council's Entertainment Officer hopes they will go; agreement in Galashiels was not unanimous. One objector argued very properly that the Edinburgh show would "take them out of their environment" would make "a publicity stunt out of the Braw Lad's Gathering".

The representation of any event as dramatic, and once as necessary for defence, as the Common Riding in one or other of its forms is not transportable, like opera or a play. It depends not only on good riding, on the bearing of the actors, but on local setting and background. It should be done as and where it has been done for years, perhaps for centuries, carrying out an act as old as the place itself. This minor battle of the Borders continues.

Galashiels in a passionate desire to be up-to-date (we shrink from the shoddy phrase "with it") proposed to hold a psychodelic dance in which, by sound and sight, the dancers or players would simulate the effect of drugs. This would, it was argued, serve as a horrid and unforgettable warning. But would it? Opponents thought that such vivid representation might well be a stimulant. The event was banned.

The town may find seemly solace in the new library, large, admirably well planned and furnished, with ample stores of books, altogether in the tradition of the reading public commended 130 years ago by the Border clergy.

The Border press reports all these matters; and always, like a rousing refrain comes a note about the battle of the Borders over planning and development.

One newspaper had a Farming Supplement in March, with one article in favour of the plan: "The picture of a booming Borders is one which many dedicated men and women are trying to achieve"; Hawick and Galashiels are seen as growing points which is fair enough. But can Hawick grow—with its hills around it? As for development and building over the countryside there is considerable opposition; a just fear among farmers of the loss of arable and pastoral land. If this is taken for building houses and factories, and more and more people are brought in to live in the one and work in the other, more and more food will be needed; but wheat does not grow between factory walls, sheep do not graze happily on small back garden-greens.

There is an account of the oldest farm on the Borders, Simprim, near Coldstream in Berwickshire, which is also one of the most modern in working and equipment. It goes back to 1686 or thereabouts, to the last of the Stuart kings. It still has its great or High Barn, built about that time, which used to store most of the grain in east Berwickshire; also to hide the cattle brought over the Border from England by the bold reivers. Modern ways began here with the introduction of a grain-handling plant. There cannot now be much room for sheltering lifted cattle; it may be as well that reiving, as a Border custom, has fallen into disuse.

From Tweedside into Ettrick and Yarrow made a pleasant

journey on an April day with plenty of sun for brilliance though hardly enough for warmth. The lion of March was still rampant, and the wind blew snell and strong. It is a genial landscape around Selkirk; the hills recede, there are low slopes, wide fields; it was all a luminous green with yellow undertones, dark green and blue-green among the trees. The lambs, born in the past two weeks or so were tiny and white beside the grey bulk of their mothers: shivering little mortals, lambswool is a fine coat but rather too fine in a gale.

> The bonny lambs wi' their canny ways,
> And the silly yowes that bleat.

That quotation from Violet Jacob heads an article in *The Southern Reporter* (by Edwin Hector) about the lambing time. Canny indeed, or clever or prudent the lambs must be if they are to survive; they must keep close to the maternal warmth. Are the yowes or ewes so silly? They may sound so in their bleating, but most of them know what they are about. In youth they are, no doubt, as foolish as the young of every species.

"A gimmer can be fikey". That statement may be Greek to the mere English, but to the Borderer, to most Scots, in fact, conveys a plain fact. The writer amplifies it: "A gimmer, a two-year-old that is, coming down with her first lamb", being young and inexperienced is fidgetty, fussy and restless. She bleats for help. One gimmer produced her lamb safely, and took to him kindly but by the afternoon had somehow mislaid him; her bleating was distracted. The shepherd understood. He found her lamb not far away, trying to make friends with other two lambs and their mother who had no use for him. Gently picked up and restored to his own parent, there was a happy mutual recognition with no further accidents. The gimmer had learned her lesson. The trouble with lambs is that however wobbly they may be on their legs, they can and do move around.

There can be sadness. Another ewe dropped a dead lamb and her cry was pitiful and bewildered. There is only one way of comfort, and that is to substitute a living lamb clad in the coat of the dead one. The shepherd skinned the little corpse:

"There's some jobs, whether you like it or not, that has to be done. The knife is aye sharp at lambing time". This knife soon had a tiny woolly coat ready for wear.

Mercifully, a neighbour had a ewe that had lambed triplets; she could deal with two, the third was gratefully invested in the woolly coat. He was hungry, and thankful to stagger across to a new mother unencumbered by rival mouths. She, forlorn, and heavy with milk, welcomed this nursling, sniffed his coat, adopted him. After a day or two the borrowed coat could be discarded. There was no memory of any loss.

The land needs care at every season of the year, but the flocks need it even more. They are living creatures, sentient, dependent at a crisis upon human skill, wisdom and tenderness. There is more than physical care here, more than a prosaic and practical aspect of shepherding. The craft goes back for countless centuries; it is one of the relationships between man and beast which have never lost kindness. It has given us some of our oldest and most memorable imagery.

Half unconsciously the mind recalls it, while the eyes look on the pastures and the sheep with their lambs. The pastoral Psalms drift through the memory, the Twenty-Third among the most loved and comforting of all. Phrases of the Old Testament recur, looking towards the Gospel fulfilment:

"He shall feed His flock like a shepherd, and shall gather the lambs in his arms; and shall gently lead those that are with young."

Handel's music has something of the tranquil nobility of this landscape.

Selkirk like all the Border towns looks to the hills, but is not, like Hawick encircled by them; the sky line is undulating, it is almost a ripple of low hills, there is almost the illusion of a landscape made by water, apart from the actual streams and river; water contours, water-colours, lucid, gentle. It is Biblical landscape in these Border valleys, Ettrick, Teviot, Yarrow and Tweed, hills and pastures all lit and interlaced by running water, living water. The hills stand about the fields and towns and lonely cottages like walls of defence. Green of many shades, flashes of blue and yellow, the gleam of silver or pewter make a palate of living and vernal colours.

Selkirk remembers the past with visible memorials. Outside the municipal buildings stands the statue of Fletcher the Souter, bearing his flag as he bore it back from Flodden; on the stone plinth are carved words poignant and plain: 'O Flodden Field'.

In the Square, the court-house bears two plaques: one commemorates the granting of the town's charter by James V, the other states:

"In this building, from 1803–1832, Sir Walter Scott as Sheriff of Selkirkshire, administered justice".

It is a good sentence, with no nonsense about it and no flurry of adjectives. Scott would have liked it. He long concealed or tried to conceal his authorship of the novels, he tried to conceal his pride (but for all that took no more kindly to criticism than do most authors, great or small), he dearly liked his new style of Laird of Abbotsford; but his first dignity, his professional office was deeply and openly valued. In this building, in this town and shire he was first of all—not the poet and novelist, the Great Unknown, the Border laird and founder of a family, but The Sheriff, chief officer and administrator of justice. His statue is high above the square, in his legal robes.

Another Border paper (there are several, and long may they flourish!) *The Kelso Chronicle and Jedburgh Gazette* reviews, with a glow of local pride added to judicial criticism, the new Life of R. M. Ballantyne—*Ballantyne the Brave*—by Eric Quayle. One did not associate this hero of young Victorians and many generations of successors with the Borders. Coral Islands, the South Seas, the Far North of the fur-traders and America of the Indians and of the Norse explorers—these are rather the regions evoked by his name. But he was born, like Scott, in Edinburgh, and like him was a true Borderer in blood and name; nephew, indeed to John and James Ballantyne with whom Scott's fortunes were so closely and disastrously linked. "I'll tell you a story" young Walter promised young Jamie at Kelso grammar school; "I'll tell you a story" R. M. Ballantyne promised many generations of boys and their sisters. The Border genius for a tale was in him too.

It may seem a far cry from Kelso to the Coral Island or the Canada of the Fur Traders; the actual journey began when young Robert Michael became a clerk in the service of the Hudson Bay Company.

His books gave the authentic, continuous thrill of excitement, of danger and adventure. Children fell upon them with delight; and parents approved without reserve, for with the thrills went morals. These books are instructive as well as entertaining. R. M. B. took great pains with every detail of background, of history and geography. His boys were brave and resourceful and they were very religious, prone to emit devout reflections; these books might almost have been permitted on Sunday.

Foulshiels, Peat Law, Langlie Hill, Ettrickbank, Philiphaugh, Harehead Hill and Harewood Glen—they all lie near Selkirk; a little further off is Newark Castle, what remains of it, on Newark Hill; not far off, too, is Bowhill in its splendour. South-west we go into the Forest, into Yarrow, to Hogg's Mount Benger, to Dryhope, Drycleugh, Henderland Hill; south to St. Mary's Loch, to Altrive, to Loch of the Lowes. A mere cata-logue of names has poetry in it. We are coming up to the source of Ettrick now, with Moffat not far to the west; we are close to Peeblesshire, to Tweedsmuir, a little out of the Scott Country.

Another day takes us to Roxburghshire again, to Jedburgh, Queen Mary's town and the county town where Scott's pleading in the courts began; whence began also those journeyings among the hills and valleys to find lost ballads.

We pass Earlston—Ercildoune—on Leader Water, in Lauder-dale; a pleasant little town, like most on the Borders, with a square in it and a garden in the square, modern and busy with its mills and its quarry, but it does not altogether forget True Thomas. The Rhymer's Tower stands near, though whether it was his abode is doubtful, according to probable of building. Into a wall of the late Victorian church is built a stone from a much older kirk, with the words: "Auld Rymr Race Lies in this Place". A tombstone in the churchyard reminds us: "Time how short Eternity how long".

On to St. Boswells, with Bemersyde on the east, the Eildons west; past Dryburgh with its Abbey in that incomparable setting of lawns and trees; Bowden on the west, Mertoun and Maxton east, then Smailholm and Makerstoun beyond. It is country all the way of hills and waters, of little towns and villages, people getting on and off the bus, going about their affairs, with greet-ings and comments in the softspoken, broad-vowelled Border Scots.

St. Boswells is like a Randolph Caldecott illustration with its houses set round the wide green, once the setting of a fair, still a centre for the Buccleuch Hunt.

"The fox jumps over the parson's gate"—we might see him at any moment, and the whole hunt streaming behind.

About two miles away is Mertoun House, designed early in the elegant eighteenth century by Sir William Bruce, the seat of the Duke of Sutherland. And if Sutherland sounds a long way from Roxburgh and the title has no Border ring about it, it must be explained that the present Duke, formerly Earl of Ellesmere, succeeded a distant kinsman in the Dukedom, his predecessor, the fifth Duke, dying without issue. The title of Countess of Sutherland with the lands in Sutherland was inherited by the late Duke's niece. The present Duke descends from a younger son of the first holder of that title who was created Earl of Ellesmere. The Duchess is a Percy, sister to the Duke of Northumberland and to the Duchess of Hamilton. By those two marriages came two new Border alliances.

The country here is almost lyrical in beauty, the hills in the background, the colours luminous under April skies. It has been a late spring but the trees are beginning to bud, and the flowers in all the gardens along the road have been dauntless. We come on past Lilliesleaf, Ancrum, Hartrigge (do any names, except perhaps those in the Gaelic Highlands equal those of the Borders?) into Jedburgh, Jeddart or Jethart on its own Jed Water which flows into Teviot.

The town has been called one of the gateways into Scotland from the south, lying on the main Newcastle–Edinburgh road, near Carter Bar, a fine centre and starting-point for exploration of the Scott Country.

The sad and lovely shell of the abbey stands above the water. Somehow there is a sadness in the air, although it is a cheerful little town enough; busy, but not as busy as it should be. The mills are still working but there are too few of them, and the work is too limited.

There is little unemployment, but that is because those who would be unemployed have drifted away, especially the younger men. Some have gone no further than Hawick and Galashiels, and are, in the modern word, commuters; but commuting does not help local shops; the cry is for more scope.

Sadness lies about the abbey as it does about any ruined church no matter how carefully preserved and cherished; it is empty of use: "bare ruined choirs" where once the Work of God was performed.

It lies too about Queen Mary's House in the heart of the

town: a small, plain house such as the Queen by no means despised. Like all her Stuart forebears she loved magnificence but also loved homeliness and simplicity. The building is strong, with thick walls, solid doors, tiny windows, a good place of defence against wind and weather as against human attack. This is Ker country, Monteviot, the home of the Kers, of the Marquess of Lothian, is near Jedburgh, and this house once belonged to a Ker of Cessford. The family were left-handed, so the twisting stair has a left-handed turn in order to let its owner thrust, if necessary, with left hand at any foe. For about forty years the house has been cherished as a memorial and museum; for a long time before that it was used as an ordinary dwelling-house. A museum, but not one of dead relics; Mary's personality is too vivid for that.

She came here to administer justice in 1566; the year of her son's birth, of her brief reconciliation with Darnley, and the final estrangement. Already she had endured many grievous things, already come near being snared; much more ill was yet to come.

There is no legend of her haunting the place, but her memory permeates it, her personality is about it. She lay very ill here, after her mad ride to Hermitage to visit Bothwell lying wounded; she came very near death: "Would God I had died at Jedford" she was to cry; if she had, there would have been a memory, a legend of a beautiful and bewitching young Queen, her life troubled and cut short; the black tragedy of her latter years would not have befallen her; the chief problem of her guilt or innocence would not have been posed.

Among the relics of her presence are a piece of tapestry worked by her and her Four Maries; a watch and thimble case; and one of infinite sanctity, her private Communion set: chalice and flagon, patten and pyx all tiny, all exquisite. Her signature—Marie R.—appears on a letter written to Ker of Cessford.

An embroidress might well copy a pattern from the garden: there are still the old pear trees—one of them was blown down in the spring gales—and they still bear blossom and fruit. The pears have little sap or substance now, and will keep only a day or so, yet they still come in their season. It is too early to see the delicate glory of blossom (or flourish, to use the pleasant Scots word); May is flourish-time. But the daffodils are golden and gay. The Burgh Flag is kept in Queen Mary's House, which would please her, ready to be carried by the Jethart Gallant at the Riding.

If we cannot at this season have local pears we can have local sweets: Jethart Snails, made from a traditional recipe. They are a dark-brown toffee curled into the shape of a snail, delicately flavoured with peppermint and are altogether delectable. Other Border towns have similar delights: Hawick Balls and Berwick Cockles among them. You pays your penny and you takes your choice, and if you have the luck to have enough pennies, you takes the lot! They are all agreeably hot, with peppermint or ginger, in the mouth.

It would perhaps be indiscreet to choose a favourite among the Border towns, if you do not happen to be a Borderer; if you are, you do not, of course, choose. Your own town is the best. The incomer or wanderer may turn with equal, or almost equal affection from Jedburgh with its abbey, lovely and sad, with Queen Mary's House and all the memories of her, the happier memories of young Walter Scott and his friends, the beauty of the countryside beyond—to Selkirk with Souter Fletcher and his banner, Scott standing on his plinth outside his court-house, the low hills around and the wide waters, Ettrick and Yarrow, the trout streams, and the salmon leap at Selkirk Cauld; to Kelso for its French grace with its market square, its great bridge, its château and its abbey; Melrose, small, compact, alert, looking to the triple cleft of Eildon, clustering round its abbey. Hawick and Galashiels are intent upon business but they do not forget their history; far from it, they re-enact it with fervour; and they too look on river and hills beyond their streets and mills and shops. They all of them carry tradition into the present. They all knew Scott, they all lie within his country; as he knew them at kirk or market, in the law court, on their rivers, up among the hills beyond them.

The pattern of life on the Borders is changing, and must still change, whether there is development at this point or that. Even without the influx of new people to work in new industries, the younger generation will not hold to the ways of their fathers. Yet the traditions which have continued, vitally, through the centuries are not dying; they are not cherished merely as old customs, they are still part of the life of each place. Each town has its character as well as its aspect; one valley differs from another; there is a local allegiance both to a town and county and to a river: a man is of Tweedside, or of Yarrow or Ettrick or of Teviot. In no part of Scotland is local character more marked, local pride more intense, historic tradition more happily integrated into everyday life. The Borders are akin to the Highlands in this, but perhaps with less nostalgia for the past.

The Borders have made the sheep or the sheep have made the Borders; have it as you will. The Border trade above all others continues to be the making of tweeds and woollens. Given those facts, development is still a matter for sensitive planning. The problems are not easy: how to retain the young after their schooling is over, or bring them back after they have qualified more fully elsewhere; how to employ them and use their full energy and amuse them; how to continue a good way of life; to welcome tourists, to make the most of all the treasures of the past without settling down in a museum or a library; how, in short to expand without distortion, to live with the present while gratefully maintaining past traditions, to live a natural, local life stimulated by tourism but not dominated by its claims; to live in the present, prepare for the future, cherishing the past and drawing from inherited experience.

One recalls the story of the boy who set off one fine morning to find the house with the golden windows that lay on the other side of the valley from his home. He walked all day and came at evening, the sunset in his face, to a house much like his own, with windows of plain glass. Turning round he saw across the valley another house of golden windows, facing the sunset, and recognised it as his own. He had seen, that morning, a house which faced east and the rising sun.

To look too long and hazily into the past may be to see golden windows; equally they may be seen if we look wishfully into the future. Some of us will always prefer to walk westward, others east. To stay, most of the time, where we are and get on as fully as possible with the business of living is for most of us necessary; we may, from time to time, have time to stand and stare—in whatever direction we choose—or to make a day's pilgrimage there and back.

The Scott Country, changed in many ways and still changing, is still easily recognisable as the land he knew. Much of the change he would accept, much no doubt, deplore. Character is not easily lost in people, in topography, in a way of life and it is still marked and strong in his country. To lose it would be tragic, an impoverishment of all Scotland. Sometimes it looks as if it were passing altogether. The young things on the Borders, like their contemporaries in the cities on both sides of those boundary hills and rivers, follow rapidly and noisily after their own strange new things. They follow like sheep, so some disgruntled critics may say. But sheep, after all, have a way of finding pasture and of coming home in the end.

EPILOGUE
Two Hundred Years After

On 15th August 1971, came the bi-centenary of the birth of Walter Scott. It was celebrated not only in Edinburgh and at Abbotsford but all over the Borders, his *ain countrie;* not only by authors, lawyers and literary historians but by a multitude of people whose knowledge of his work ranged form having heard about him and having had to learn a poem and read a novel of his at school, to being constant and intimate readers. His fellow Borderers had very properly a special pride in his memory, for he was one of themselves.

For Abbotsford and the Borders the commemoration began long before the birthday; by Easter, visitors and tourists were flocking to the house and the countryside: individuals, small groups, large parties from schools and societies all over Scotland, from over the Border, from beyond the seas. Americans came in floods. The culmination of course was reached in August; and on the eve of the birthday, the beacon fires were lit on the hills, and one on Arthur's Seat; Abbotsford and Melrose Abbey were floodlit with the effect of near-magic loveliness, a vision that lingers in the mind. 14th August was a day and evening of dim skies and recurring rain, a contest between the elements of fire and water. But the fires were not quenched.

On Sunday there was a commemorative service in the Kirk of Greyfriars where Scott's father was an elder, and one that evening in Melrose; at both were Scott's great-great-great-grand-daughters. In the afternoon Her Royal Highness the Duchess of Gloucester, herself a Scott of Buccleuch, opened the Exhibition in Parliament House. In this, and at Abbotsford itself, one seemed to come closest to Scott, the whole man; for here, in one of the courtrooms he sat as Clerk to the Court — his chair is carefully kept. He was a lawyer in his bones; the law, more than a livelihood to him, helped to form his mind; it enriched him with a knowledge and experience which his genius could transmute.

This exhibition was arranged by a committee representing

three bodies: the Court of Session, the Faculty of Advocates, the National Library which is the son and heir of the former Advocates' Library. Here were gathered books and manuscripts, documents, portraits, landscape paintings, a visible biography. There was space to wander, look, linger and return.

The city's exhibition, *Writer to the Nation*, in the Waverley Market, was also rich in visible records. Its illustrations to the novels with their dramatic backgrounds and its miniature scenes were all presented in an atmosphere of Gothick gloom or twilight, at once romantic and slightly comic, which would have amused Scott himself, and delighted Miss Catherine Morland and her creator Miss Austen who shared a zest for 'horrid' and Gothick novels.

A tiny exhibition—of a charm not to be measured by size— was presented in Melrose; a collection of figures from the poems and novels, and of Scott himself and his family, made and dressed with meticulous period accuracy, by the artist, Anne Carrick. To call this *enchanting* would not be exaggerated. It was a diminutive drama. Here were Scott himself as a small boy, with his loving and beloved Aunt Jane; Scott the grandfather with his adored Johnny Lockhart for whom he wrote the *Tales*; a foursome—with a charming Sophia and Lockhart clearly falling in love, a no less charming Anne with, alas, no sweetheart but only a brother to squire her. Meg Dods and Jeanie Deans were there; Meg Merrilees and Michael Scott; and, truly enchanting, the White Lady of Avanel, and Thomas the Rhymer lying under the Eildon Tree looking up at the Queen of Elfland in her green gown, riding her milk-white steed. Here, that first Saturday afternoon, came a group of children from the Edinburgh Central Library's children's room (itself a place of treasures) with a sympathetic librarian.

Libraries and bookshops were full of Scott's own books, of books about him and about the Borders. There were lectures, conferences, concerts and parties. A one-day conference was held, in the University, one Saturday in February, with lectures on Scott and his place in other countries; his influence on Italy, France, Germany, and Ireland. Without praising one more than another, it may be permitted to mention the engaging Irishry of the Irish lecture. It was stated in effect that Scott had little if any influence there, and what he had was to be deplored.

A major conference opened on 16th August, until Saturday of that week: with daily lectures except on Wednesday when members made a tour of the Borders (or of the Rob Roy country as they chose) and were entertained to a folk-concert or ceilidh in the evening; but every day was enlivened by some gaiety: a tour, a reception at the Castle or in the City Chambers, a dinner in the University.

This was an international gathering; the lecturers came some of them from America (Dr. Edgar Johnson, author of the massive new *Life of Scott* among them), from Ireland, from Hungary; our ain folk were there too, from university, Parliament House (Lord Clyde, President of the Court of Session) and National Library (Professor Beattie, a good Borderer).

Earlier in the year there had been two parties at Abbotsford, one in April, the other in June, organised by the Sir Walter Scott Club; guests sat in the library to hear Meta Forrest and Ian Gilmour recite scenes from the novels, passages from the poems. Their programme was given during the commemoration period itself, in Gladstone's Land in the Lawnmarket, with the Saltire Society as hosts.

And there were concerts: Lady Scott's Drawing-Room, held in the restored and lovely Saint Cecilia's Hall, down in the Cowgate, where Edinburgh's concerts began more than two hundred years ago, before the New Town was planned. The music was such as would have been performed at a party in 39 Castle Street; the Scots songs and tunes the host himself loved best and which his daughters played or sang to him; the modish Italian music they themselves liked; a Schubert setting to two of the songs in *Lady of the Lake*, and one from Donizetti's *Lucia di Lammermoor* (which was, alas, omitted from the Festival opera that year).

Scottish P.E.N. celebrated this greatest of Scottish authors by a dinner where the speeches were few but good; the food and wine excellent: the former inspired by the cookery book of Mistress Meg Dods, the latter a sound claret.

This is by no means a full account of the bi-centenary. That would itself demand a volume. Like any good treat or festival it has left not only memories but tangible and readable reminders; new books (see the bibliography) much journalism in the Border papers, in magazines, and in a special edition of the *Week-end*

Scotsman for Saturday 14th August; copies of this with other mail were delivered to Abbotsford, thence, on Sunday afternoon, carried by mail coach to Melrose post-office, there to be stamped or franked. The coach, as in Scott's day, carried passengers as well as mail; and these may be regarded as personifications as well as persons in their own right.

Mrs Maxwell-Scott was herself and also Scott's descendant and representative; two journalists represented, respectively, *The Scotsman* and *The Glasgow Herald*. The Postmasters of Edinburgh and of Melrose were there, joined by two postmen. Finally there was Corrie: there have always been dogs at Abbotsford, and this small West Highland terrier of much strength of character had no notion of letting a coach drive off without her. Corrie, indeed, stole the show.

The mail coach linked Edinburgh with Melrose as in the days before the railway (now, unhappily, closed). It was a figurative as well as an active link. And that number of *The Scotsman* was devoted to articles about Scott or reviews of books about him, his background and period.

Without incurring an odour of comparisons one might mention with special delight the essay by David Stephen on the Dandie Dinmont terrier, written in good Border Scots: "Scott invented a border farmer, name of Dandie Dinmont, and syne discovered he had invented the Dandie Dinmont terrier"—an entirely credible claim for Scott who had more creative energy than he well knew what to do with and could invent a dog in the by-going. The Dandie Dinmont was happily described by David Stephen as "a mouls dichter"—with nose so near the ground that it dusted or wiped the mould or earth.

Of the books reviewed in that issue (and of others during the year) again one may be chosen: *The Blue Heaven Bends Over All* by Jane Oliver: her last, and alas, a posthumous novel.

Here is presented vividly and truly, Scott the whole man in his every aspect and activity: from smallest boyhood at Sandy-knowe with his grandfather's sheep and their shepherd, to the autumn day at Abbotsford where he lay dying, in the great bay window that looks upon Tweed, the sight and sound of it the last his senses could receive; the huntsman's horn pealing out as he departed, as if all the trumpets were sounding for him on the other side of the river of death.

The bi-centenary celebrations had many virtues: variety, scholarship, colour, music, fun and feasting. If one word must be chosen it would be *life*. They celebrated a living memory, a living tradition in a living world of today that would not appear altogether strange to him.

Edinburgh and the Borders share the honours; but perhaps we might dare to say that this celebration made the city and capital part of the Borders and that many good Borderers would think that was Edinburgh's crowning glory.

BIBLIOGRAPHY

Books about the Borders are as many and varied as the Border burns. This is by no means a complete list, but it contains those mentioned in the text and others. Books are like streams and waters and byways; one leads to another and the journey is delightful.

Sir Walter Scott comes first: in his novels, especially *Guy Mannering* and *The Black Dwarf*; his own poems, especially the Introductions to the longer poems; his *Minstrelsy of the Scottish Border*; his *Journal* (edited by J. G. Tait, published by Oliver and Boyd); his *Letters* (in the Centenary Edition by Grierson, Cook and Parker, published by Constable); and the *Life* by J. G. Lockhart.

The poems, tales and autobiography of James Hogg, the Ettrick Shepherd, are full of Border lore and legend; as are the *Memorials of James Hogg*, edited by his daughter Mrs. Gardner (published by Gardner of Paisley). His *Domestic Manners of Sir Walter Scott* show himself as well as his subject.

The poems and ballads of the Borders may be found in many anthologies: *The Oxford Book of Ballads; The Edinburgh Book of Scottish Verse* (edited by W. Macneile Dixon); *The Northern Muse* (edited by John Buchan and published by Nelson); *A Scots Anthology* (edited by John Oliver and J. C. Smith, published by Oliver and Boyd); and *The Oxford Book of Scottish Verse*.

John Leyden may be found in his *Poems* and *Ballads*, with a *Memoir*.

The Reverend Dr. Thomas Somerville published *My Own Life and Times;* this, with the *Letters and Memoir of Mrs. Alison Cockburn* and the Leyden and Hogg may not easily be found except in a major library, but are well worth the search. So too are the *Border Essays* and the *History and Poetry of the Scottish Border* by John Veitch, and the *History of the Border Counties* by Sir George Douglas.

History, told by contemporary observers with a knowledge

of the past is told in *The New Statistical Account of Scotland* pub-
lished by Blackwood in 1845; and in its modern successor the
Third Statistical Account now in process of publication by Collins.
The latter, in the account of Selkirkshire, gives due praise to *The
History of Selkirkshire* by Thomas Craig-Brown.

The *Tales of the Borders* collected by John Wilson are fascinating
and valuable, whether in the original many-volumed edition, or
the volume of selections published by the Moray Press.

Among books of yesterday and today the following are much
to be commended:

Andrew Lang: *Angling Sketches; Adventures Among Books* (both
  published by Longmans).
            The Gold of Fairnilee (recently republished by
  Gollancz).
Jean Lang: *Land of Romance; North and South of Tweed* (T. C. and
  E. C. Jack).
W. S. Crockett: *The Scott Country* (A. and C. Black).
J. B. Selkirk: (James Buchan Brown): *Poems* (published in
  Selkirk).
Stewart Cruden: *The Scottish Abbeys* (Her Majesty's Stationery
  Office).
John Buchan: *Sir Walter Scott* (Cassell).
            Scholar Gipsies (John Lane).
            Memory Hold the Door (Hodder and Stoughton).
George Burnet: *Companion to Tweed.* (Methuen).
John Geddie: *The Scott Country* (Blackie).
Madge Elder: *Tell the Towers Thereof* (Robert Hale).
Kathleen Fidler: *Flash the Sheep-dog* (Lutterworth).
Eric Quayle: *Ballantyne the Brave* (Hart-Davis).
The Shell Guide to Great Britain and *The Shell Guide to Scotland*,
the latter written by Moray McLaren (both published by Ebury
Press and George Rainbird) contain excellent sections on The
Borders.
Arthur Melville Clark: *Sir Walter Scott, The Formative Years*
  (Blackwood).
A. O. J. Cockshut: *The Achievement of Sir Walter Scott* (Collins).
David Daiches: *Sir Walter Scott and His World* (Thames &
  Hudson).
D. D. Devlin: *Sir Walter Scott, of Waverley* (Macmillan).
Edgar Johnson: *Sir Walter Scott, The Great Unknown* (Hamish
  Hamilton).

Sir Tresham Lever: *Lessudden House: Sir Walter Scott and the Scotts of Raeburn* (The Boydell Press).

Moray McLaren: *Sir Walter Scott, Man and Patriot* (Heinemann).

Jane Oliver: *The Blue Heaven Bends Over All* (Collins).

INDEX

A

Abbeys, *see* Dryburgh; Jedburgh; Kelso; Melrose
Abbotsford, 13–15, 32–7,112,117, 136–7,148–9,153, 181, 183–4
Arthur, King, 39–42
Ashestiel, 27, 31–2, 137

B

Baillie-Hamilton Family, 159–63
Ballads, 46–53
Ballantyne, James and John, 18
Ballantyne, R. M., 174–5
Border Development Scheme, 121, 148–56
Border families, *see* Baillie-Hamilton Family; Douglas (Douglas Home) Family; Elliot Family; Haig Family; Kerr Family; Scott Family
Borders, The:
Festivals, 71–2, 109–10, 113–18, 170
Place names, 14–15, 175
Religion, 54–63, 82
Towns, 64–82, 106–22, 169–78
Brown, John Buchan (J. B. Selkirk), 97–9, 103
Brown, T. Craig, 100, 106, 113
Buccleuch, Duke of, *see* Scott Family
Buchan, Anna (O. Douglas), 135
Buchan, John, 131–5
Burnett, George, 14

C

Cockburn, Alison, 94–5, 100
Cruden, Stewart, 61
Cuthbert, Saint, 54–9

D

Dickinson, William Croft, 41, 43
Douglas (Douglas Home) Family, 38, 166–8
Douglas, O., *see* Buchan, Anna
Douglas, Rev. Dr., 32, 95, 108
Douglas, Sir George, 38, 56
Drummelzier, 16, 40
Dryburgh Abbey, 24–5, 60–61

E

Edinburgh, 16, 18, 20, 72, 85–7, 92, 94, 105, 120–21, 130, 149–50, 181–5
Elliot, Baroness, 164
Elliot Family, 95, 164
Elliot, Jean, 95
Ettrick, River, 13, 16, 96, 128, 173
Ettrick Forest, 47, 51, 53, 95
Ettrick Shepherd, The, *see* Hogg, James

F

Festivals, *see* Borders, The
Fidler, Kathleen, 143–4
Flodden, 77, 95, 99, 113, 173

G

Galashiels, 14–15, 32, 76–7, 106–112, 148–54, 156, 178